MAKING YOUR OWN Teddy Bear

PEGGY & ALAN BIALOSKY AND ROBERT TYNES

Photographs by Jerry Darvin

Illustrations by Susan Gaber

Workman Publishing
New York

Library of Congress Cataloging in Publication Data

Bialosky, Peggy.
Making your own teddy bear.
1. Soft toy making. 2. Teddy bears. I. Bialosky, Alan. II. Tynes, Robert. III. Title.
TT174.3.B53 1982 745.592'4 82-60061
ISBN 0-89480-212-7
ISBN 0-89480-211-9 (pbk.)

Art Director: Paul Hanson
Designer: Charles Kreloff

Cover photographs: Jerry Darvin
Additional Photograph: Ideal Toy Corp., page 6
Teddy Bears, wardrobe, and accessories designed and executed by Robert Tynes

Workman Publishing Company, Inc.
1 West 39 Street
New York, NY 10018

Manufactured in the United States of America
First printing October 1982
10 9 8 7 6 5 4 3 2

DEDICATIONS

For both of our mothers, all of our bears, and for Suzanne.

Peggy & Alan Bialosky

For Violette Declaive, my mother, who by her guidance, inspiration and example, opened to me the world of creative fantasy. This book could never have been without her existence.

Robert Tynes

ACKNOWLEDGMENT

To Suzanne Rafer, our editor, our very deepest appreciation and sincere gratitude for her endless patience and limitless help and assistance.

CONTENTS

TEDDY BEAR BASICS

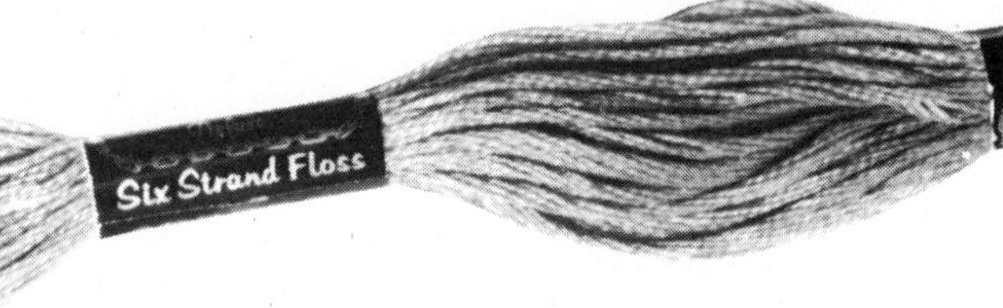

TEDDY BEAR CONSTRUCTION

TEDDY BEAR WARDROBE

TEDDY BEAR ACCESSORIES

THE TEDDY BEAR FAMILY

Meet the Teddy Bear family in full color, with all their clothes and accessories. Papa is featured between pages 16 and 17, with a Teddy Bear Identification Tag and Luggage Tag for you to photocopy. Mama appears between pages 32 and 33, with a Teddy Bear Registration Certificate. You'll find Baby between pages 80 and 81 along with a place to paste a photo of the first Teddy Bear you complete.

TEDDY BEARS

THE TOY WITH A HISTORY

You are about to make a treasure: your very own Teddy Bear, or better yet, your very own family of Teddy Bears.

The toy you have chosen to make has a history. While blocks and balls may have less specific origins, the Teddy Bear appears to have sprung from an event in United States history.

In 1902 President Theodore Roosevelt was on a hunting trip in Mississippi. As reported in *The Washington Post,* the presidential hunting party trailed and lassoed a lean, black bear, then tied it to a tree. The president was summoned, but when he arrived on the scene he refused to shoot the tied and exhausted bear, considering it to be unsportsmanlike.

The following day, November 16, Clifford Berryman, *Washington Post* editorial cartoonist, immortalized the incident as part of a front-page cartoon montage. Berryman pictured Roosevelt, his gun before him with the butt resting on the ground and his back to the animal, gesturing his refusal to take the trophy shot. Written across the lower part of the cartoon were the words "Drawing the Line in Mississippi," which coupled the hunting incident to a political dispute.

The cartoon drew immediate attention. In Brooklyn, New York, shopkeeper Morris Michtom displayed two toy bears in the window of his stationery and novelty store. The bears had been made by his wife, Rose, from plush

This later version of the Berryman cartoon appeared in The Washington Star.

stuffed with excelsior and then finished off with black shoe-button eyes. Michtom, recognizing the immediate popularity of the new toy, requested and received permission from Roosevelt himself to call them "Teddy's Bears."

The little stuffed bears were a success. As demand for them increased, Michtom moved his business to a loft, under the name of the Ideal Novelty and Toy Company. This same company exists today, grown into the modern Ideal Toy Corporation.

At the same time as it was born in the United States, the Teddy Bear was also born in Germany. The Steiff Company of Giengen produced its first jointed stuffed toy bears during this same 1902–1903 period. The company had been toymakers for a number of years and had produced little wool-felt pincushion-type animals which included elephants, donkeys, horses, pigs and camels. These were the creations of Margarete Steiff, whose charming toy animals had first delighted neighborhood children, then children and adults of many lands. The first Steiff Teddy Bears were introduced at the 1903 Leipzig Fair, where an American buyer saw them and ordered several thousand for shipment to the United States.

While other stories and tales have been told regarding the birth of this wonderful toy, the apparently simultaneous births in Brooklyn and Giengen are the best substantiated. The most wonderful part of this story is that the Teddy Bear's appeal to children and adults has never stopped growing. Now you too will be adding your name to this ongoing history.

An original 1903 Ideal Teddy Bear.

TEDDY BEAR BASICS

Embroidery Thread & Fabric

Stuffing Materials

Glass Eyes and Alternatives

Bear Supplies

Stitch Dictionary

EMBROIDERY THREAD & FABRIC

All the bears in this book were made using a jersey-backed fur fabric which gives them a real bear look. Other suitable possibilities are almost endless; they work very nicely in velvet or velveteen, textured wool, felt, cut or uncut corduroy. Even the fuzzy wrong side of a sweatshirt could be used.

The paw pads and bottoms of the feet should be cut from a different material than the rest of the bear. If fake fur is used for the bear, the paws could be of flannel, felt or velveteen in a matching or even a contrasting color of your choice.

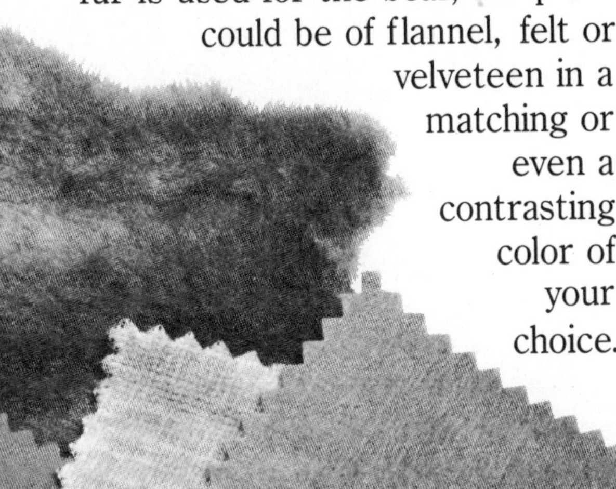

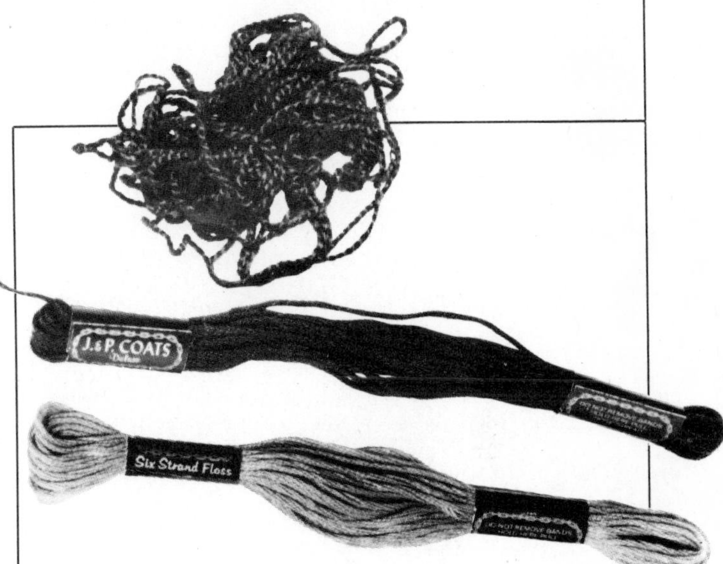

Although regular embroidery thread was used to make the nose and mouth of the bears in this book, you may wish to use silk twist (floss). This is neither widely available nor is it usually found in colors other than white or natural. Therefore it would have to be dyed beforehand.

If you do decide to use silk, remember *not* to boil the floss during the dyeing process since boiling takes out the luster. Start with cool water, add the dye, and when it is well mixed, add the silk which you have predampened. Slowly bring it to a simmer and continue to simmer until you have the desired color. Leave it to cool in the dye bath overnight, then remove it from the bath, rinse it in cool water and hang it to dry over a clothesline (never use a wire hanger; it could rust your silk).

STUFFING MATERIALS

There are endless materials that can be used for stuffing, from old stockings to feathers and straw. The three main stuffings, however, are: kapok, cotton batting and, in the last few years, polyester fiber.

KAPOK: This is a fine fiber obtained from the seed pods of the ceiba tree. Kapok has a nice silky feeling and it does not get lumpy when used as stuffing, but it is very expensive and difficult to obtain in many places. Most kapok is now imported from England (see the mail-order section, page 111).

COTTON BATTING: This is just regular cotton, the kind used in the making of quilts. It is quite easy to find and is not too costly. Its greatest drawback is that it lumps up *very* badly into hard balls if one is not extremely careful, when used for stuffing.

POLYESTER FIBER: This is the most widely used stuffing material today. It usually comes in 16-ounce bags, and it is cheap and found almost everywhere. There are almost no drawbacks except that it makes the items stuffed kind of bouncy and it can lump up a bit.

Whatever material you use for stuffing, it is a good idea to pull the material apart a bit before you use it. This breaks down any lumps and puts air into the stuffing material. Also, try to keep it in "sheets" which you can ease into position rather than balling it up and jamming it into place—this only makes lumps and hard areas. A stuffed object should have an overall firm quality and be smooth. There is nothing worse than seeing a lumpy surface with hollows all around the lumps. Stuffing, like everything else, takes time to master and one must work with slow care. It all adds up to giving a work a professional look rather than a badly made "homey" look.

GLASS EYES AND ALTERNATIVES

Many of the old bears and animals have shoe-button eyes or ones made of glass. Glass eyes give the animals a wonderful "alive" quality and that is what was used for our family. But they do have drawbacks; they are rather costly, not always easy to find, and they do break. If you are making a bear as a toy for a very young child, glass eyes are not the safe choice. Instead, acrylic eyes that come with lock washers should be considered. Before the bear's head is stuffed you just push the shank through your material and then place the lock washer onto it *(Fig. 1)*. This holds it firmly. Circles of felt, stitched securely, may also be used as eyes, or you may wish to embroider the eyes, using a satin stitch. Since these could not be pulled off, perhaps they would be the safest version.

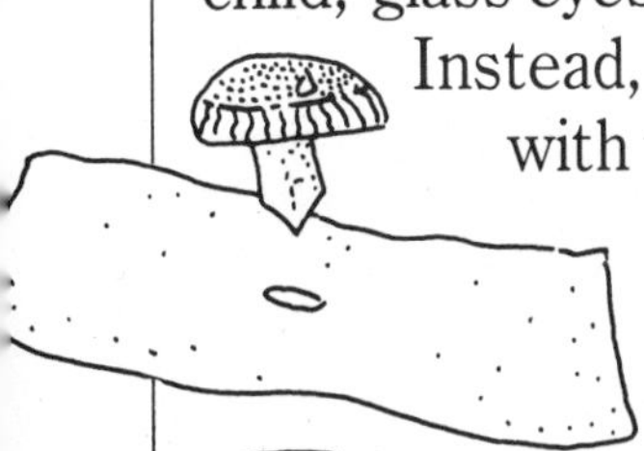

Fig. 1

Glass eyes are sold according to millimeter diameter. They come in two ways and either is fine to use. Some have rounded wire shanks already embedded in them and are ready to sew on. The second kind comes as a length of wire about 4 inches long with a glass eye attached to each end of the wire. You will need wire cutters and a pair of long-nosed pliers to cut and form the necessary loops so that you may secure the shankless eyes into your bear.

1

Cut the wire in half *(Fig. 2)*.

Fig. 2

2

Use the pliers to make a small loop and twist the wire end around the shank to hold the loop tight *(Fig. 3)*. Clip off any excess wire.

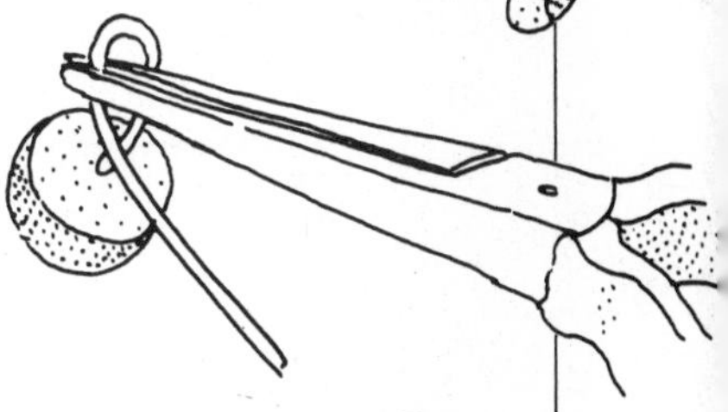

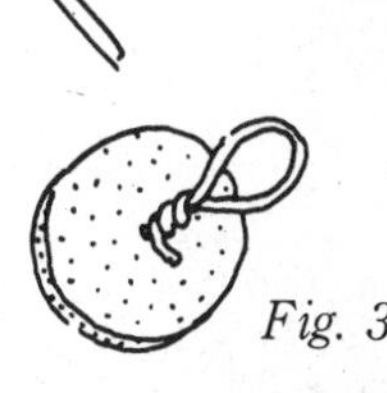

Fig. 3

16 mm glass eyes with preformed shank

14 mm glass eyes mounted on wire

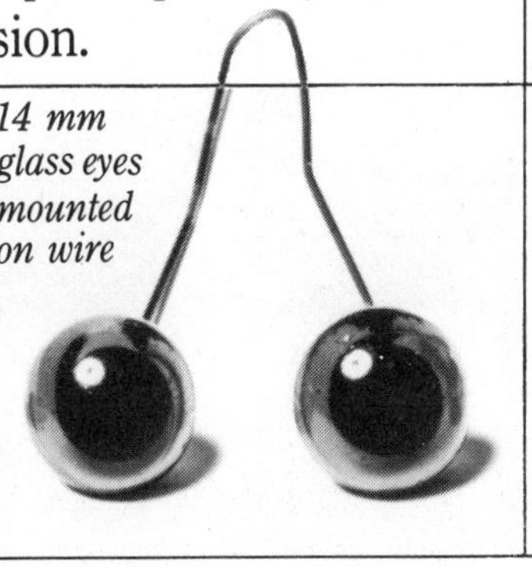

12 mm glass eyes

Safety eyes with washer lock

BE
SUPP

Single-edged razor blade for cutting out the pages for the Flower Book.

Long-nosed pliers for making crown joints and bending eye shanks.

Tracing paper to trace patterns from the book.

Scissors for al cutting. It is preferable to have one for fabric a one for paper

Oaktag and thin cardboard for making patterns.

Metal ruler, pencil and felt-tip pen for measuring and marking.

AR
LIES

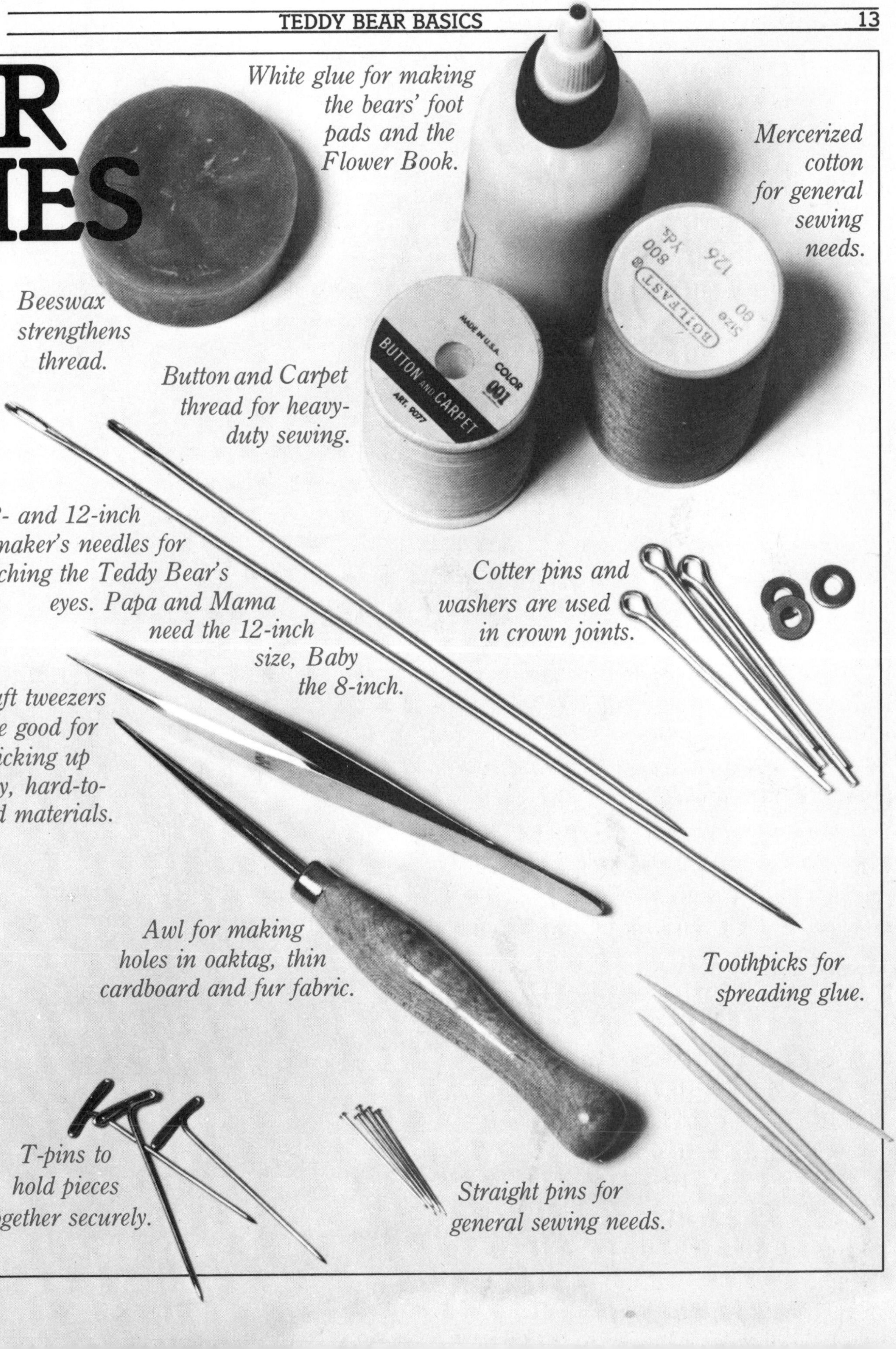

White glue for making the bears' foot pads and the Flower Book.

Mercerized cotton for general sewing needs.

Beeswax strengthens thread.

Button and Carpet thread for heavy-duty sewing.

8- and 12-inch toymaker's needles for attaching the Teddy Bear's eyes. Papa and Mama need the 12-inch size, Baby the 8-inch.

Cotter pins and washers are used in crown joints.

Craft tweezers are good for picking up tiny, hard-to-hold materials.

Awl for making holes in oaktag, thin cardboard and fur fabric.

Toothpicks for spreading glue.

T-pins to hold pieces together securely.

Straight pins for general sewing needs.

STITCH DICTIONARY

There is quite a bit of hand-sewing required to complete the bear family and their clothes. In fact, the entire family can be sewn by hand, if you prefer.

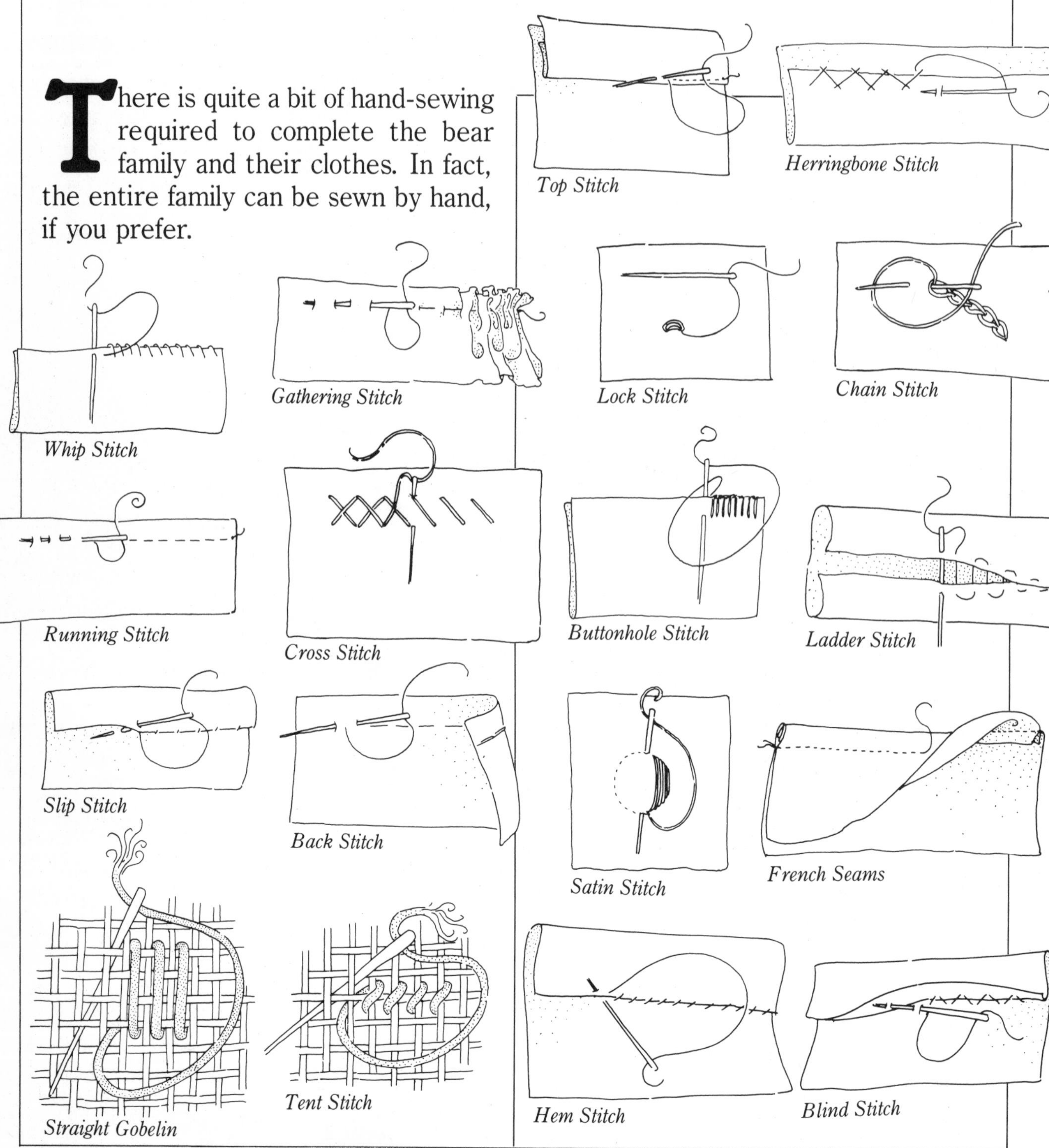

Top Stitch

Herringbone Stitch

Whip Stitch

Gathering Stitch

Lock Stitch

Chain Stitch

Running Stitch

Cross Stitch

Buttonhole Stitch

Ladder Stitch

Slip Stitch

Back Stitch

Satin Stitch

French Seams

Straight Gobelin

Tent Stitch

Hem Stitch

Blind Stitch

TEDDY BEAR CONSTRUCTION

Bear Beginnings

Crown Joints

Patterns

Cutting Out the Bears

Assembling the Bears

Attaching the Limbs

Stuffing the Bears

Designing the Face

Papa Bear

Mama Bear

Baby Bear

PAPA BEAR

A good-natured dreamer who loves flowers.

Papa is named Bayreuth, a grand, opera-inspired name. He was created as somewhat of a dreamer, and with an interest in flowers and honeybees. At all times he carries his book of pressed flowers and is always adding to the collection. His jacket sweater has a Tyrolean look and he sports a large nosegay. A crisp white collar and a floral necktie finish the ensemble. The fur fabric used to make Papa is a slightly darker shade of honey than that of his mate.

Some of the rough sketches used in designing Papa's outfit.

Papa's colla

The floral print tie picks up on the flower theme.

The jersey-backed fur fabric us in making Papa.

Papa's sweater is cut from an old, large crew neck. To give it a Tyrolean effect, the front pieces are cut on a curve, and a nosegay of artificial flowers and some small brass-looking buttons have been added.

Papa's book of pressed flowers.

The flowers in Papa's book include:
Honesty
(Lunaria)
Narcissus
(Amaryllidacea)
Periwinkle
(Vinca minor)
Shadbush
(Amelanchier canadensis; *shown above)*
Violet
(Viola)

Papa, the largest of the three bears, measures 17 inches in height.

TEDDY BEAR IDENTIFICATION TAG & LUGGAGE TAG

Have both the identification tag and luggage tag photocopied from the book. Glue the tag onto white oaktag, plasticize it (if possible), then tie it around your Teddy Bear's neck using ribbon. Once photocopied, the tag may be tied directly onto your bear's suitcase, hat box, tote bag, trunk or even attache case.

BEAR BEGINNINGS

Just a few words before you start. With very few exceptions, the materials used in making the Teddy Bear family and their wardrobe and accessories come from the five-and-ten. Many things you will perhaps find around your home; others will have to be bought. Besides the suppliers listed (page 111), a good place to look for odds and ends of all sorts is your local thrift shop. Here, if one has an open eye, all kinds of treasures may be found.

Once gathered, arrange your supplies and materials so that you will know just where to find everything. If you are lucky enough to have a small workroom or storage space it is important to devise a kind of filing system. This will save time and allow you to make full use of your work space. Place all your flowers, laces, ribbons, buttons and trimmings in separate marked boxes. This way you can see at a glance just what you have and whether a special purchase must be made. And it will help greatly in speeding along your projects since you will not be wasting time digging around for scattered materials.

One of the major ingredients necessary for the completion of the projects in this book is patience. These are not difficult projects but you must be prepared to devote time to complete each of them. The bears themselves are more or less "fixed" outside of fab-

ric choice, and minor things such as different eye treatments and alterations to the size and shape of the feet and paws. With the clothing, though, there can be plenty of variation. The basic garments are very simple to cut and sew up. It is only in the trimming and the materials used that they might become complicated and time-consuming. It is wise, also, to keep in mind that even if the patterns and designs are followed exactly, there is always a difference . . . as no two things ever turn out quite the same. This is one of the most exciting aspects of creative work—each piece has its very own personality, even when one has used the same patterns, fabric and trimmings. This is especially true with the making of bears.

As everyone knows, bears are wonderful companions and marvelous listeners, but they really do have very definite ideas on how they want to look when you make them up. Do not be surprised to discover that no two ever look alike, no matter how hard you may try! Each and every bear has its own personality. Why fight it, they always win! After all, it is just your job to stitch them together; the rest they will take care of themselves. Once a bear is completed, check the size of its clothes patterns to make certain the fit is correct before starting. You may have ended up with a willowy bear—in which case the measurements will have to be adjusted down—and then again it might have turned out to be a portly one!

One last but very important thing to keep in mind: Many of the things incorporated in the making of these bears could prove harmful to a young child. The bears' glass eyes or the small buttons and flowers used as trimming on the bears' wardrobe, for instance, aren't safety-secured and therefore do not meet with the Federal Hazardous Substance Act. Some alternative suggestions have been offered but it will be up to the good judgment of each individual to see to the elimination of all hazardous parts included in the directions, if the bear is being made for a child.

CROWN JOINTS

Crown joints are an indispensable necessity for making jointed bears. In most old bears the joint disc was made of wood, sometimes of heavy cardboard, and occasionally of tin.

The easiest thing to do, of course, is to order the ready-made joint sets (see suppliers list, page 111). Or if you wish, you can make your own. All three bears in our family use the same size joints, which measure 1½ inches across. Each set is made up of 2 wooden or hardboard discs, 2 small metal washers, and 1 cotter pin (see photograph).

If you decide to make your own, the steel washers and cotter pins may be purchased at most good hardware stores. Cotter pins come in different lengths; the ones that are 2 or 2¼ inches long are easier to work with than shorter ones. (If they are too long they can always be cut down.) They come in different thicknesses; choose the thinner ones for easier bending. Do remember to check the size of the metal washer opening since you do not want the head of the pin to pass through the washer.

The discs, which are 1½ inches across and about ⅛ inch thick, can usually be purchased at craft stores. (They are often referred to as hardboard washers.) If they cannot be found, they can be cut from a dowel stick or made from cardboard circles glued together to the desired thickness. The cardboard discs are not very durable, though, and are best used on smaller bears.

HOW TO MAKE CROWN JOINT DISCS FROM WOOD

Should you decide to make your own wooden crown joint discs, use a dowel stick 1½ inches in diameter. You will need only one since they are sold in a standard 36-inch length. A local hardware or lumber store should stock them. For each bear you will need eight ⅛-inch-thick discs. The lumberyard might cut the discs for you or you can cut them yourself.

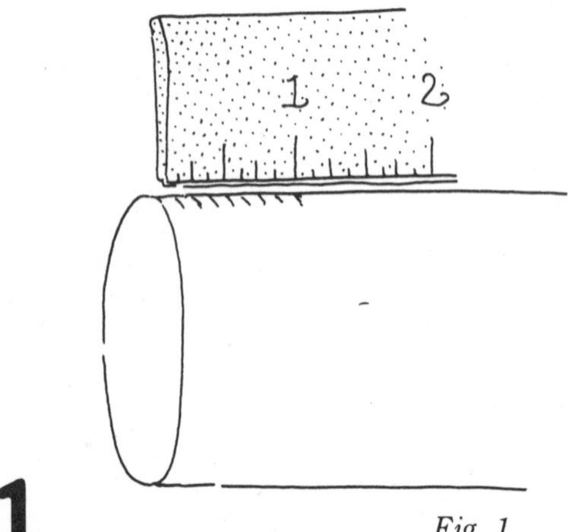

Fig. 1

1

Starting at one end of the dowel, mark off ⅛-inch intervals until you have the desired number of discs *(Fig. 1)*.

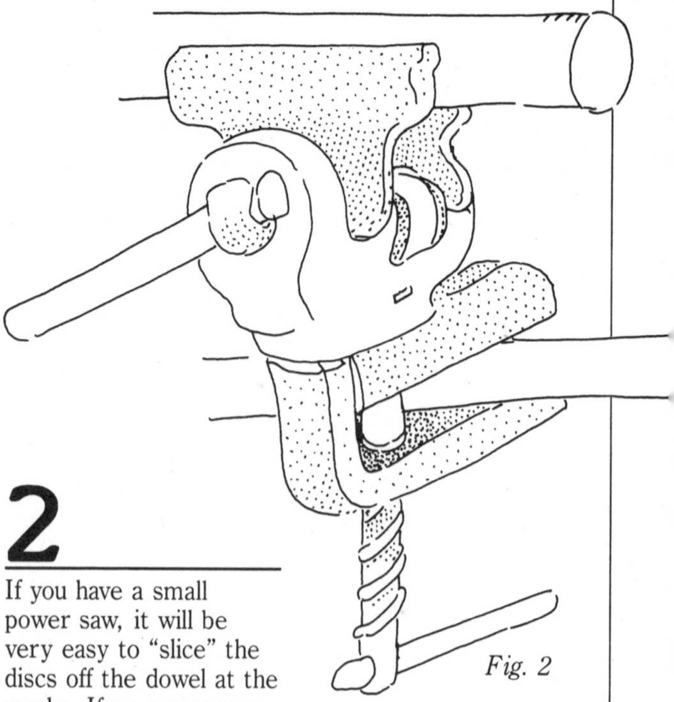

2

If you have a small power saw, it will be very easy to "slice" the discs off the dowel at the marks. If no power saw is available, you will need a small vise and a small handsaw. Clamp the dowel into the vise behind your last mark, and saw off one disc at a time *(Fig. 2)*. If your discs turn out to be slightly thicker or thinner than ⅛ inch, do not worry; they will still be usable for your joint sets.

Fig. 2

3

When you have cut out all your discs, sand them, using a medium-grade sandpaper. The flat surface of the discs should be smooth. As the last step, you will need to drill a ⅛-inch hole in the center of each disc *(Fig. 3)*.

Fig. 3

HOW TO MAKE CROWN JOINT DISCS FROM CARDBOARD

If you decide to make your discs from cardboard, the number of layers you will need will depend on the thickness of the cardboard. You can use scraps and small pieces—such as the backs of little note pads, tissue boxes or other types of boxes—so long as you can cut it easily with a pair of scissors. The scraps should measure about 2 x 2 inches. Besides the cardboard, you will need a pair of scissors and white glue.

DISC PATTERN

1

Following the directions on page 24, trace the disc pattern from the book. Then transfer it to oaktag or thin cardboard, remembering to mark the center hole. Cut out the first disc *(Fig. 1)*.

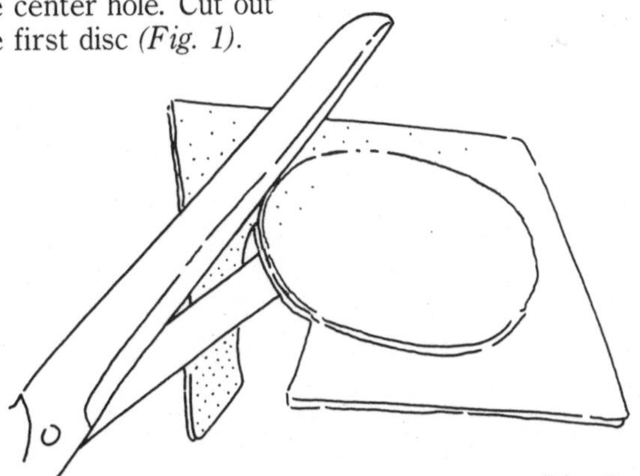

Fig. 1

2

Take another piece of cardboard and place it on a small piece of waxed paper measuring about 4 x 5 inches. Take the disc you have already cut out and cover the entire surface of one side with a thin coat of white glue. Place this disc, glue side down, on top of the piece of cardboard you have placed on the waxed paper. Cover with another piece of waxed paper, weight it down and leave to dry.

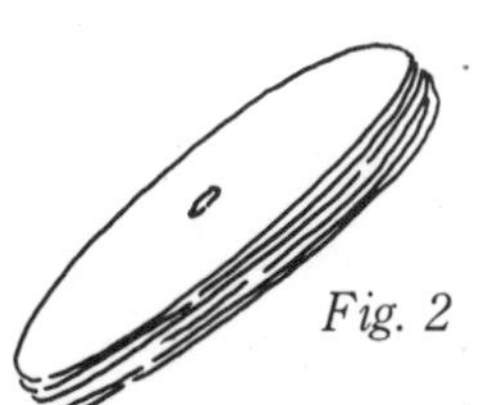

Fig. 2

3

When dry, pull away the sheets of waxed paper. Using your scissors, cut away the excess from the layer of cardboard that you have glued to the cut-out disc. Continue to glue on layers of cardboard, allowing each to dry and then cutting away the excess. It may take 5 or more layers before you reach a ⅛-inch thickness *(Fig. 2)*.

4

When the disc is at least ⅛ inch thick, mark the center hole and, using a drill and a ⅛-inch bit, drill the hole through the disc. Continue making discs in the same manner until you have completed 8.

5

If you wish to make your cardboard discs somewhat stronger and longer lasting, paint each disc all over with a coat or two of white or orange shellac, allowing the shellac to dry between coats.

GETTING THE TENSION RIGHT

Once you have the pieces assembled, making your own joint is not difficult—but you must practice doing it using scrap fabric. You will soon get the knack. It takes only a few moments to make the crown, and after practicing on a half-dozen cotter pins you will be able to tell (to *feel*) if a joint is a successful one without even trying it out. Do not feel that since it is such a simple operation, it is one that can be left until you are actually doing the bears themselves. If you do, you will discover that the arms and legs are not tight, but instead hang limp. If they start out limp they will only loosen even more with time and wear.

The secret to making the joint is getting it good and tight. The discs should be extremely difficult to move once the joint is completed. To test, take hold of each piece of fabric and try to move them back and forth. If they slide easily, the joint is too loose, and when your bear is stuffed the limbs will have no tension and will not stay in position. So, if your material does slide back and forth, remove the cotter pin and start over again. Use a new cotter pin, as the first one will be weak and too bent to straighten out and reuse. Once you master the tension trick and the fabric hardly moves, you will be ready to go on to doing your bear's joints.

When you have completed the task of attaching the arms and legs to the bear's body, it is ready to be stuffed. Once the bear is stuffed, and the resulting tension forces the body and limbs together, your bear's arms and legs will slide nicely back and forth and still remain where you place them.

Do not be discouraged if your first several attempts are failures. Just keep practicing.

HOW TO MAKE A CROWN

After you have assembled the joint (described in "Attaching the Limbs," page 33) you will find you have a sandwich made of a metal washer, hardboard disc, the two layers of fabric you are joining together, another hardboard disc, and finally another metal washer. Through the center of these runs a cotter pin which must be correctly bent to keep the joint firm. During the crown-making process, use your free hand to hold all the pieces tightly together. To bend the crown you will need a pair of long-nosed pliers.

1

Using your fingers or long-nosed pliers, separate the 2 halves of the cotter pin slightly (*Fig. 1*).

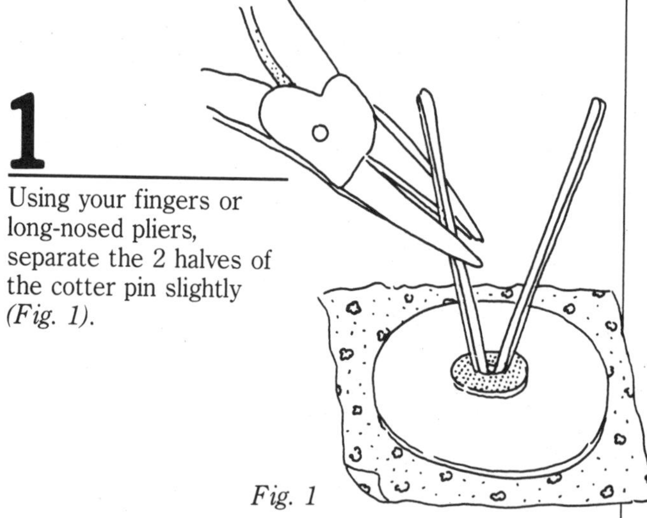

Fig. 1

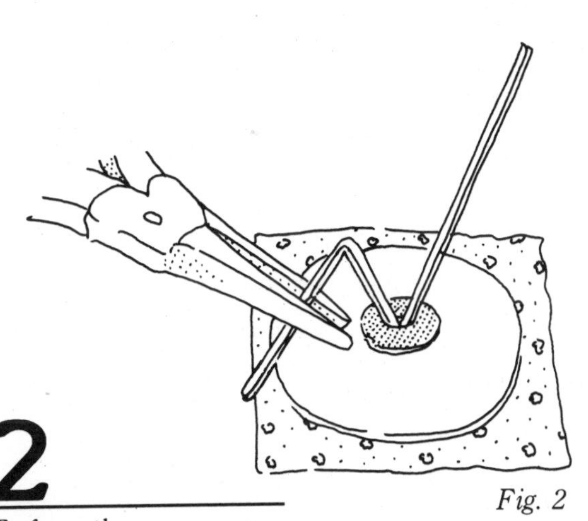

Fig. 2

2

To form the crown, grasp one of the halves of the pin about two thirds of the way down with your pliers and bend it as if to form a loop *(Fig. 2)*.

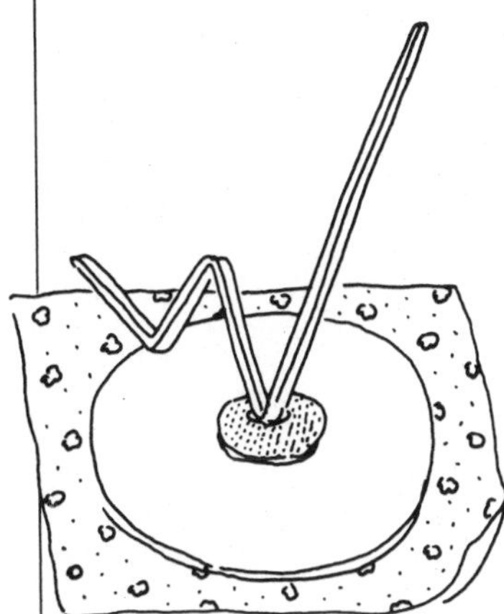

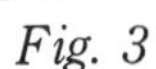

Fig. 3

3

Move the pliers about one third of the way in from the pin tip and bend the end up *(Fig. 3)*.

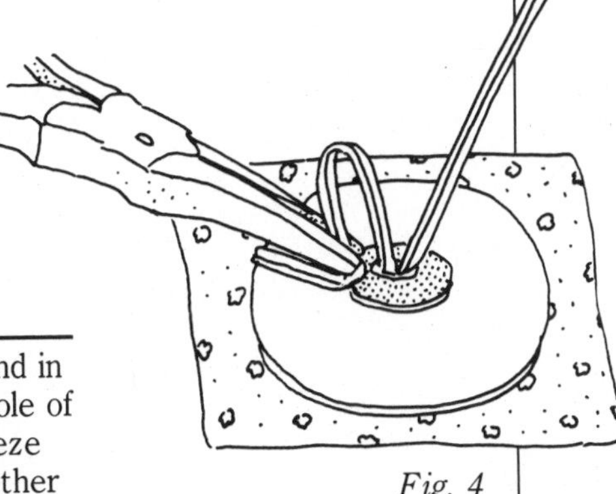

Fig. 4

4

Push the second bend in toward the center hole of the joint, then squeeze the loop tightly together at the base. It should look like half of a bow *(Fig. 4)*.

5

Flatten the loop slightly, pushing it outwards, then repeat the loop process with the other half of the pin. The finished crown should look like *Fig. 5*.

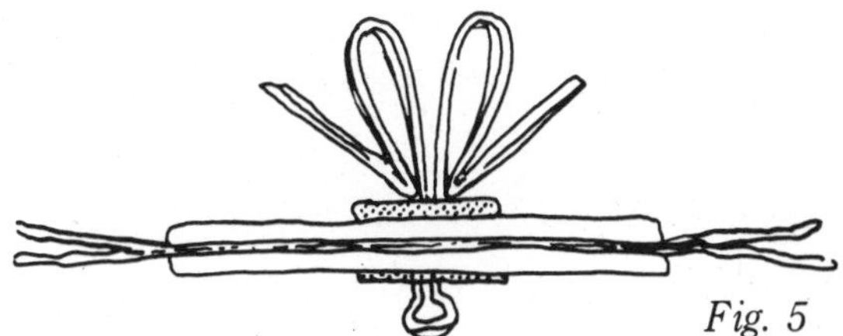

Fig. 5

6

Try moving the joint discs. If you can barely move them, the joint is made correctly. Once inside the bear, a tightly made joint keeps the limbs from flopping around. When a bear with well-made joints hugs you, you stay hugged!

PATTERNS

All the bear patterns in this book are shown actual size. Whenever possible this is also true for the wardrobe and accessories patterns. Those pieces that are too big to fit full size in this book are drawn smaller and to scale. "How to Enlarge a Pattern" is explained on page 25.

MATERIALS NEEDED

- Pad of tracing paper
- Pencil, well sharpened
- Oaktag or thin cardboard
- Carbon paper
- T-pins (optional)
- Scissors
- Felt-tip pen
- Awl

HOW TO TRACE AND TRANSFER A PATTERN

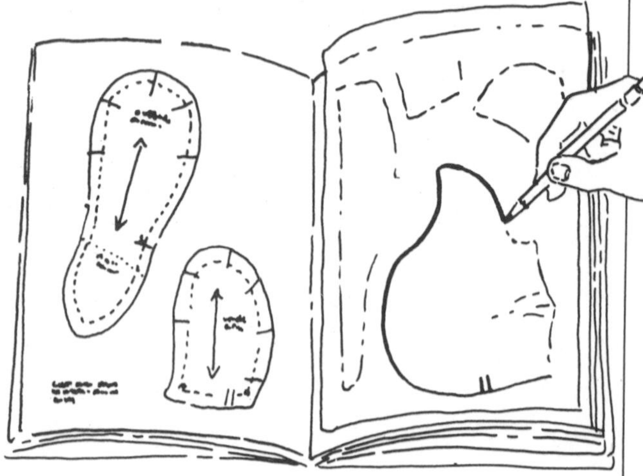

Fig. 1

1

Place a sheet of tracing paper over the pattern in the book. Using your pencil, carefully trace the pattern onto the tracing tissue *(Fig. 1)*. Transfer *all* markings to the tissue.

2

When you complete the tracing, put the book aside and place a sheet of oaktag (or thin cardboard) on your flat work surface. Over the oaktag place a sheet of carbon paper and, on top of the carbon, the tissue tracing. You might wish to tack down the 4 corners of the 3 sheets of paper to help keep them from slipping; use T-pins or tape.

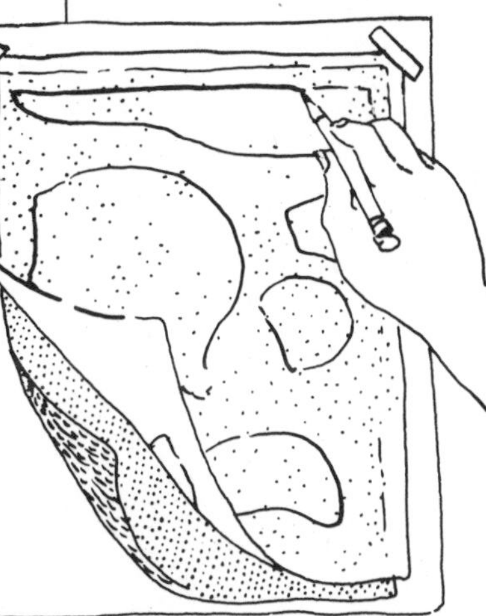
Fig. 2

3

Using your pencil, trace all around the pattern, pressing hard *(Fig. 2)*. (But be careful not to use too much pressure, as the tissue might tear.) When the tracing is complete, remove the tissue and carbon paper.

4

Using your scissors, cut out the oaktag pattern along the traced line. When you have cut out all the pieces, use a fine felt-tip pen to copy *all* the marks, notches, fabric grain lines and whatever else might be noted on the pattern *(Fig. 3)*. Also note the name of the pattern piece and what it is from, such as Papa bear/ arm.

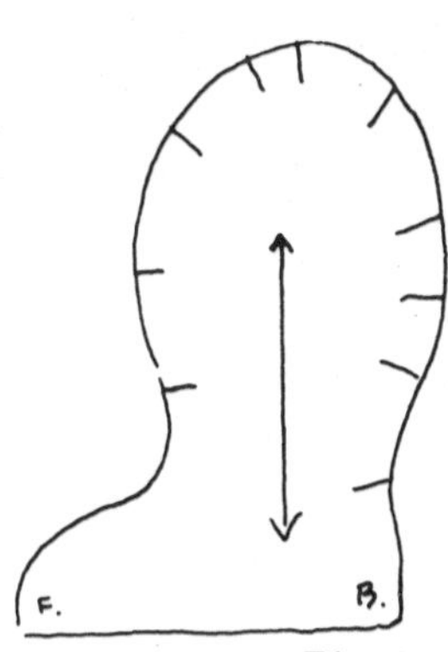
Fig. 3

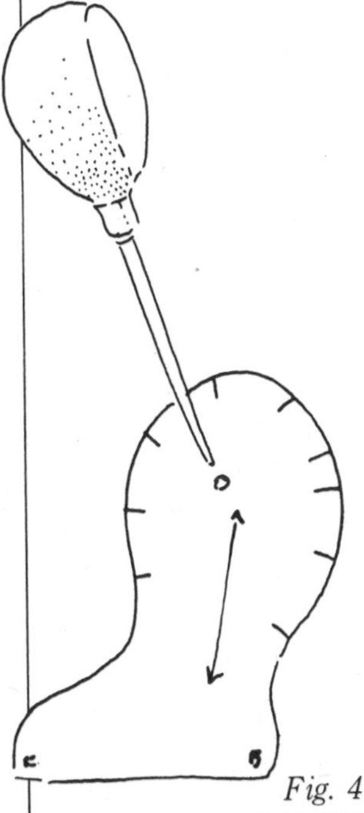
Fig. 4

5

Now, using the tips of your scissors, cut a small notch out of the oaktag at each notch mark along the edge of the pattern pieces. If there is a mark in the middle of the pattern, use your awl to punch a hole through the oaktag, being careful not to rip it *(Fig. 4)*.

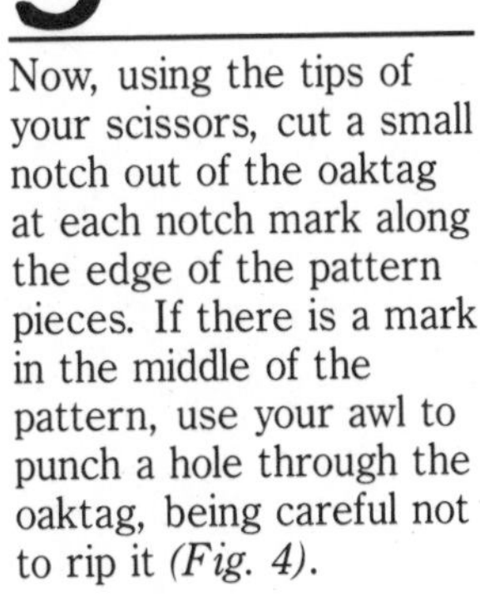

6

For each pattern you should have an envelope in which to store the various pieces. This keeps you from mismatching pattern pieces. The pattern name should be written on each envelope along with the number of pieces that go with the pattern.

Note: As mentioned before, if the instructions call for tissue patterns, not oaktag, just skip those steps and cut out the tissue pieces.

HOW TO ENLARGE A PATTERN

All the pattern pieces not traceable from the book are drawn on grids so that one book square equals one inch.

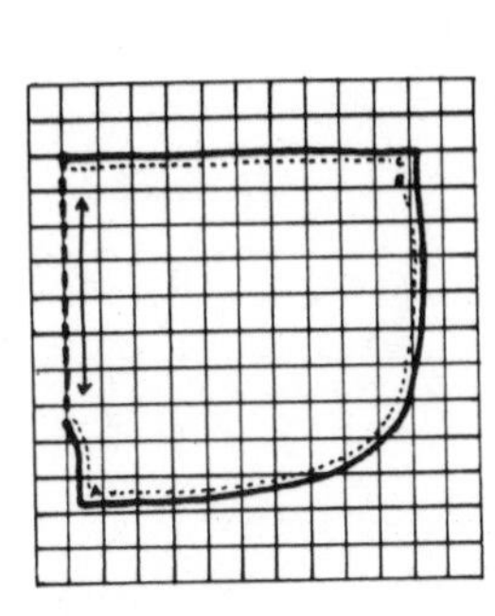

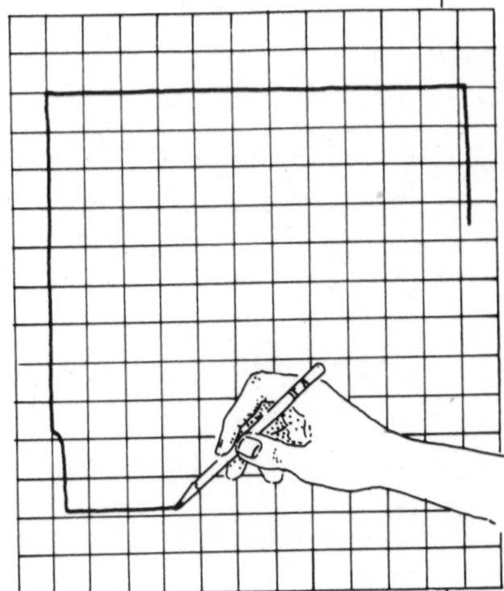

1

On a sheet of white paper rule a grid large enough to include one box for every box shown in the book.

2

Carefully transfer box by box the pattern from the book onto your paper, taking extra time to get the curves exact.

CUTTING OUT THE BEARS

The secret of good sewing is really in good cutting, so go slowly remembering *not* to pull, stretch and generally "torture" your fabric into doing things it is not able to do.

These general directions for cutting out the bears will serve for all three. Once you have completed the cutting, just turn to the directions for assembling the bear. You will see that, except for size differences, Papa, Mama and Baby are made exactly the same way.

All the fabric pieces include a ¼-inch seam allowance; do not trim any closer. Also, do not notch the fabric by cutting. Use your pen to mark in notches.

Note: Two pattern pieces make up Papa's center head piece (#2). Cut out the smaller (back) section and place it on the larger center piece, lining up the fold sides and the two sets of *X*'s. Tape them together so that they form one piece, and transfer this to your oaktag.

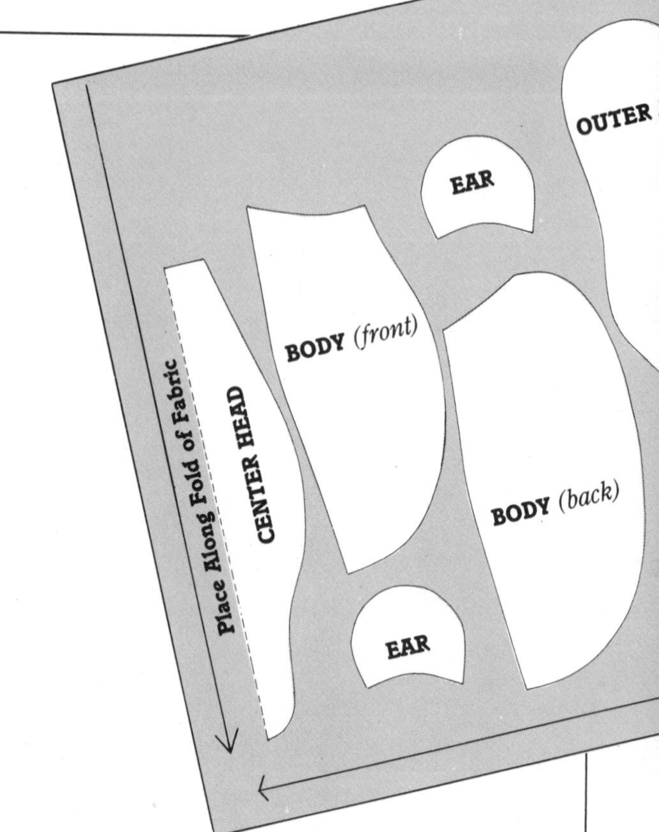

1

Lay the fabric, wrong side up, on a flat, smooth surface. Following the illustration above, lay out all the pattern pieces (except for the paws and foot pads), making certain that the arrows correspond to the grain lines of the fabric and the pile of the fabric is running from top to bottom.

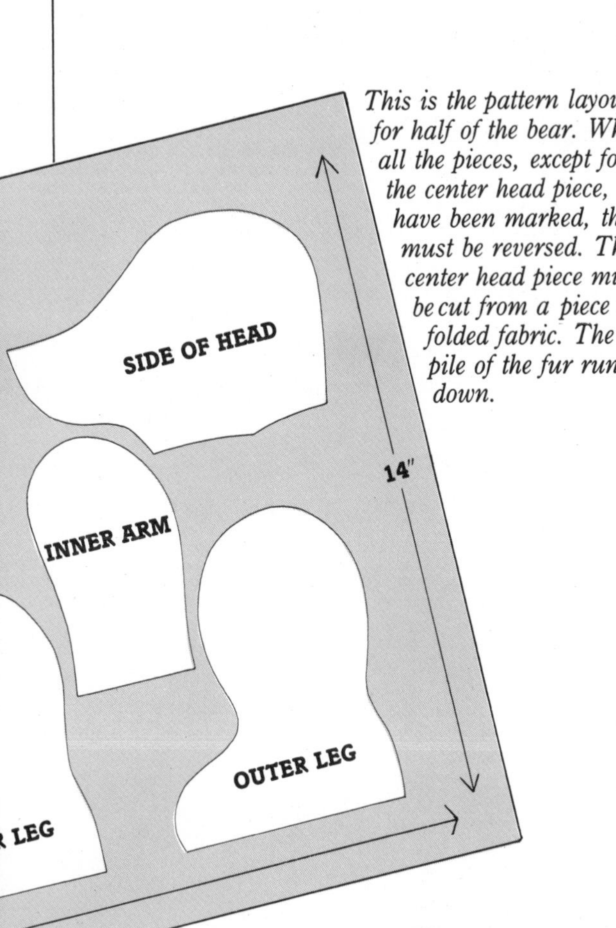

This is the pattern layout for half of the bear. When all the pieces, except for the center head piece, have been marked, they must be reversed. The center head piece must be cut from a piece of folded fabric. The pile of the fur runs down.

2

Using a black felt-tip pen, carefully trace around the pattern pieces, marking all the notches and holes. With the exception of the center head piece (#2), *all* the pattern pieces must be reversed in order to complete both the right and left sides of the bears. Once you have finished tracing around each piece, reverse it and trace around it again. You should now have a right and left side for your bear.

3

Carefully cut out the fabric, keeping the pieces that make up the various body parts together.

4

Next lay out the material you have chosen for the paw pads and feet bottoms. Place the pattern pieces on the fabric and trace around; then lift the pieces, reverse them, and trace around them once again. Cut out the pieces.

5

To make the foot bottoms firm, you must back them with notebook-weight cardboard. Using the pattern for the foot pad liner, cut out the liner, reversing and cutting out for the second pad. Be sure to mark each foot with the *B*, *F* and center line.

6

Take a fabric foot bottom and turn it wrong side up. Center the cardboard piece on the fabric, markings facing up, so that you have a ¼-inch fabric allowance all around the cardboard. Using a toothpick, spread the glue around the cardboard edges and fold the fabric allowance over the cardboard as in the photo below. Make sure the fabric is pulled tight enough so that the foot bottom is smooth, but not so tight as to buckle the cardboard. Cover the glued side with waxed paper, place any heavy object on top to weight it down, and leave it to dry. Repeat the process with the second foot bottom.

ASSEMBLING THE BEARS

A couple of sewing hints before you start: All the basting threads you use through the construction of the bears will have to be removed. This is a tedious job if done all at once so remove them as you finish each part of the body. If you are sewing the bears by hand, use a small back stitch (see page 14). If you are using a machine, set the stitch gauge at 7 or 8. Once a seam is sewn, *never* iron the fur.

Now, let's get started. You'll find the patterns and materials lists for Papa, Mama and Baby beginning on page 42.

Note: On the illustrations in this section, dots are used to indicate the wrong side of the fur.

THE HEAD

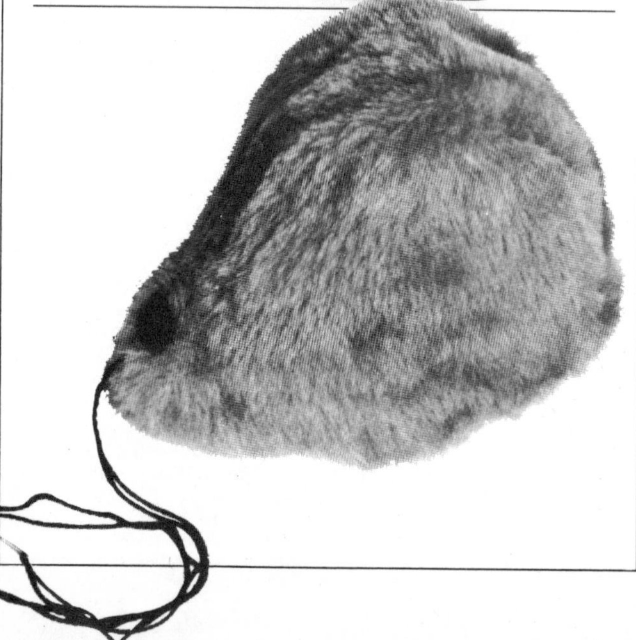

1

Take the center head piece (#2) and run a length of thread through the mark on the nose tip. Tie off very loosely. (This is done so you will be able to find the center after it is covered when the nose is embroidered.) Repeat the thread marking at the back center mark *(D)* and through both eye markings *(Fig. 1)*. Do not leave the threads too long or they will get in the way.

2

Using a different color thread, mark the ear placement.

Fig. 1

3

Using the shape on the pattern as a guide, pencil in the nose on the wrong side of the fabric. Cut a 24-inch length of the black embroidery thread or silk twist. Thread a tapestry needle, using all 6 strands of the embroidery thread. Knot one end. Working from the wrong side of the fabric, use a satin stitch to embroider the nose *(Fig. 2)*, keeping it about 1/16 inch from the fabric edge. Do not pull the thread too tightly and do not let it twist around.

Continue working the nose in satin stitch until complete, ending on the wrong side of the fabric. Knot the thread and clip off the excess. Set this piece aside for the moment.

Fig. 2

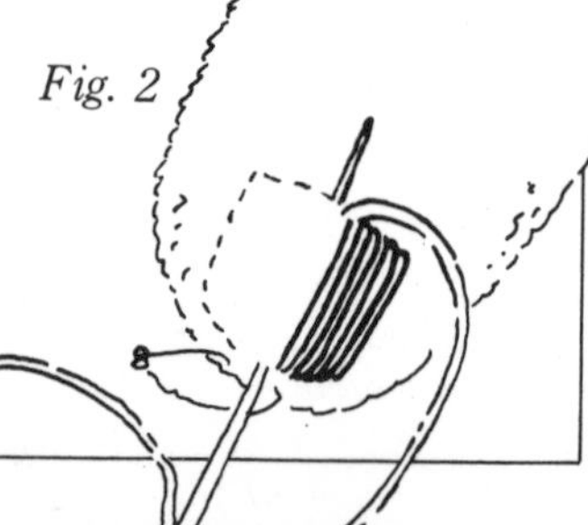

4

Mark both of the side head pieces with thread at the ear marks. Use the same color thread you used for the ear marks on the center piece. On both of the side pieces machine-stitch the neck dart on the wrong side of the fabric. Cut the darts open partway *(Fig. 3)*.

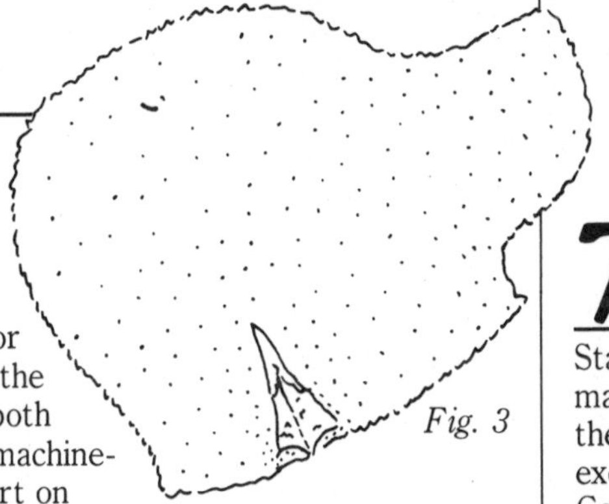

Fig. 3

Fig. 4

5

Place the 2 side pieces together, pile side to pile side, and pin along the front from *A* to *C (Fig. 4)*. Leaving a ¼-inch seam allowance, sew along the pinned front. Use a 7 to 8 stitch size on your sewing machine and be sure to lock-stitch at the beginning and end of the seam.

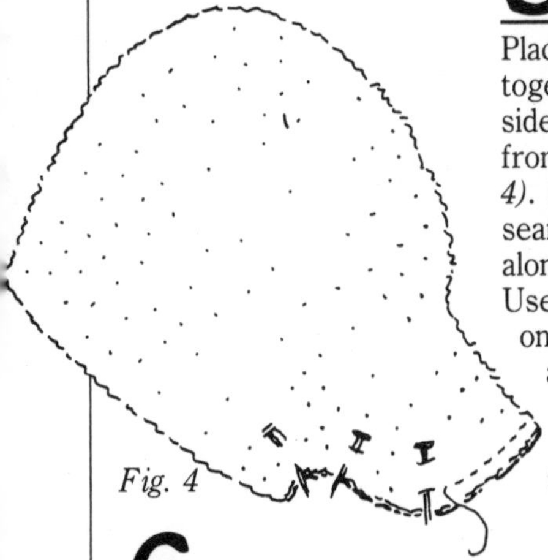

6

Take the center head section, pile side down, and match *B* on each of the stitched-together side pieces (which also have the pile facing inside) with the *B*'s on the center section. Starting at the back of the head, pin the center to both side pieces as far as the first set of notches *(Fig. 5)*. Line up the nose marking thread on the center piece with the *C* mark on the sewn side pieces. Pin the pieces together, first on one side and then on the other, easing in the fabric at the curves until you have the center piece completely pinned to the side pieces. The 3 sections now form the head of the bear. You are now ready to stitch it all together to form one piece.

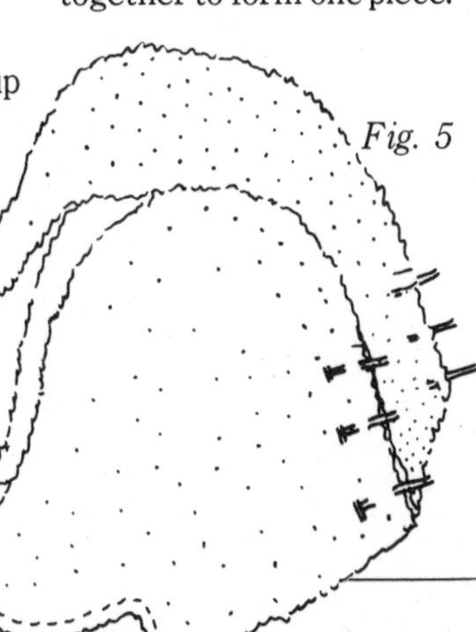

Fig. 5

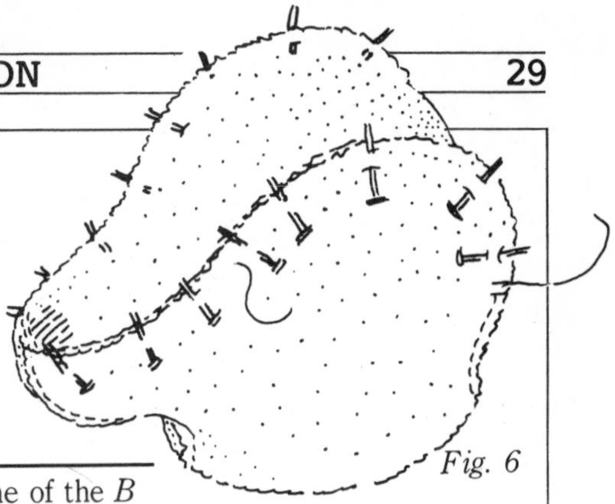

7

Starting at one of the *B* marks, machine-stitch the head, easing in any excess material *(Fig. 6)*. Continue to stitch along the seams until you reach the second *B* mark. Be sure to leave only ¼-inch seam allowance and lock stitches at both ends. Go slowly when sewing up the head, as it is important to keep the curve lines smooth. Since the side pieces are larger than the center section, you must be careful to ease in the fabric and not to let it form tucks.

Fig. 6

9

If you are using acrylic safety eyes, attach them now at the eye marks (see page 11).

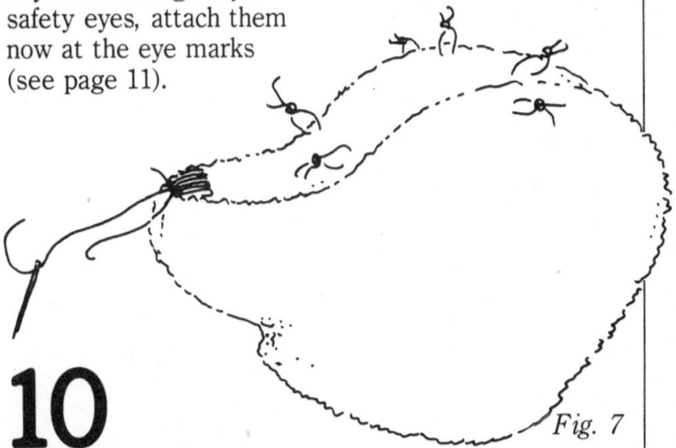

8

Turn the head so the right side is facing out. Thread your tapestry needle with a 24-inch length of embroidery thread. Double the thread and knot the ends together. From the inside of the head, run the threaded needle through to the outside just under the nose *(Fig. 7)*. Pull the thread completely through and clip off the needle, leaving the thread hanging loose until later. (One of the last things you do, after the bear is stuffed and put together, will be to sew the mouth on, using this thread.)

Fig. 7

10

Fold under ¼ inch at the neck and pin all around. Using beeswax, wax a length of carpet thread. Use it doubled to run a gathering seam all around the neck, near the folded edge. Use a small running stitch. Begin at the center front seam and end back there. Pull to tighten the thread slightly and tie off, pushing any extra thread up into the head where it will be hidden. The basic head shape is now finished.

THE BODY

1

There are 4 body pieces. With the pile facing in, match up a front and back piece. Pin them together along the side seams. Match up the second pair of front and back pieces and again pin the side seams. Machine-stitch the side seams, leaving a ¼-inch allowance and lock-stitching the seam at the beginning and end.

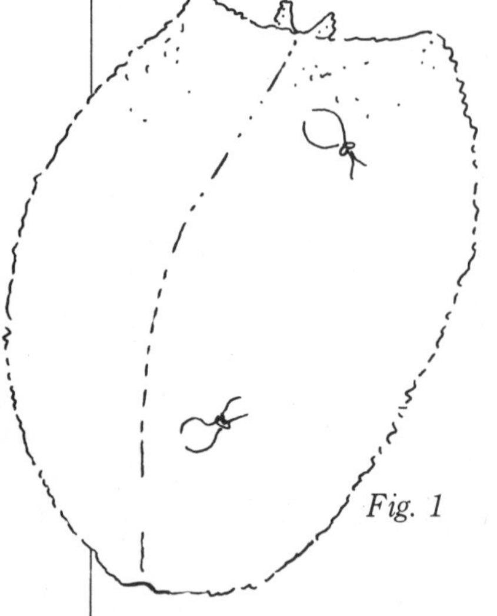
Fig. 1

2

Open both body sections. At all 4 arm and leg marks, run a knotted thread from the front to the back and back to the front again, making a loose loop. Cut the needle away and tie each loop loosely *(Fig. 1)*. These loops mark where the arms and legs will go.

3

Place one half of the body, pile side up, on your work surface. Place the second body section, pile side down, on top of it, lining up the edges so they are flush with each other all around the body. Pin the 2 pieces together, starting at *D* and continuing to *E*. At *E* make sure side seams align, one over the other. Both seams should be opened out as you pin. Do not pin past the *X* mark. Machine-stitch the 2 parts together from *D* to *X*, using a ¼-inch seam allowance *(Fig. 2)*. Lock the seam at both ends.

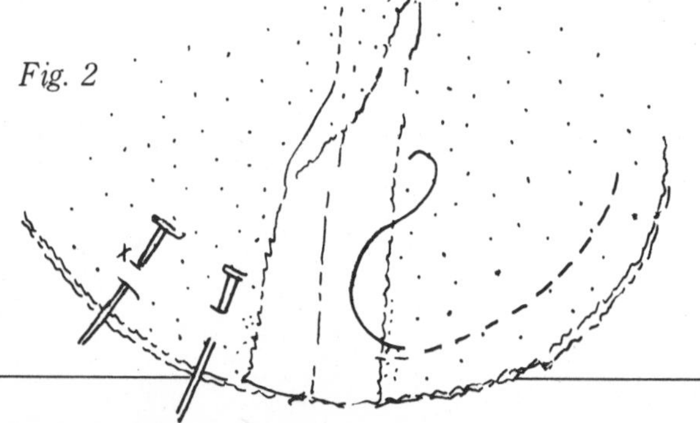
Fig. 2

4

When the stitching is completed, turn the body pile side out. Starting on one side of the body at *X*, fold ¼ inch of the raw edge of fabric to the inside, pinning as you go. Repeat on the second side. Baste along the fold from the neck to the *X* mark and back up the other side to the neckline *(Fig. 3)*. Next fold under ¼ inch of raw fabric all around the neck and pin. Wax a length of carpet thread, and using it doubled, stitch all around the pinned edge starting at one side of the front opening and ending at the other. Use a small running stitch. Leave the thread hanging loose at both ends, but you can cut the needle off. Double-check to make certain all 4 arm and leg marks have been marked on the front side with the loops of thread. Put the body aside.

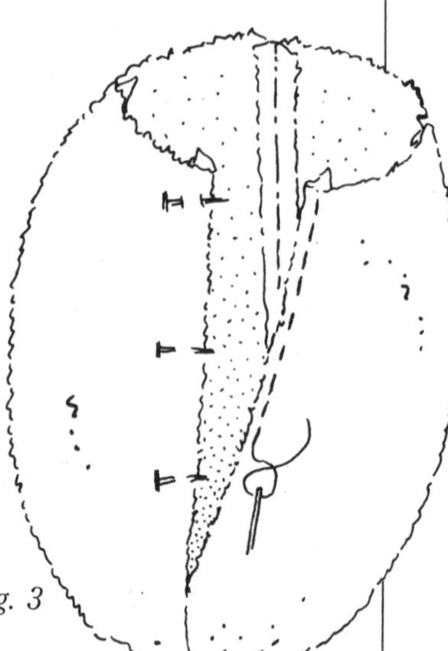
Fig. 3

THE ARMS

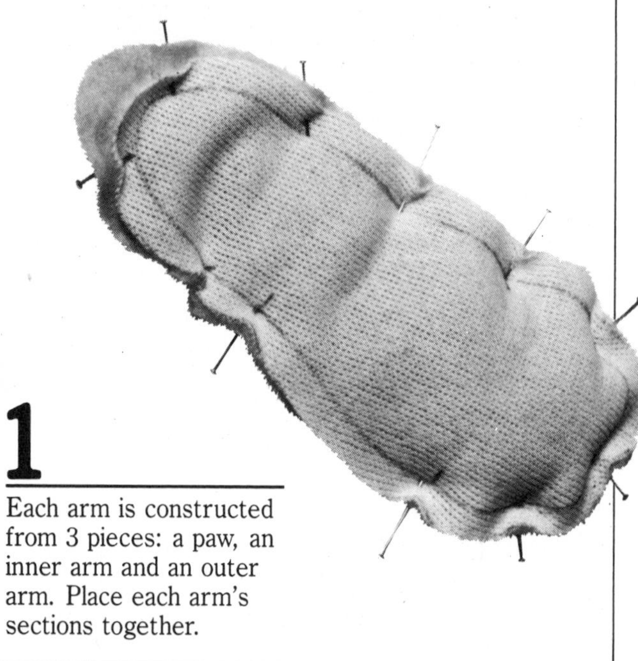

1

Each arm is constructed from 3 pieces: a paw, an inner arm and an outer arm. Place each arm's sections together.

2

Start with one arm. Lay the under arm section flat, pile side up. Place the paw piece, right side down, on top of the inner arm, matching the *Y* and *Z* of the paw with the *Y* and *Z* of the arm. Pin the pieces together. This should put the straight edge of both pieces flush *(Fig. 1)*. Locking the seams at both ends and leaving a ¼-inch seam allowance, stitch the paw and arm together. Stitch a loop of thread through the joint mark on the under arm piece as you did on the body (see page 30, step 2).

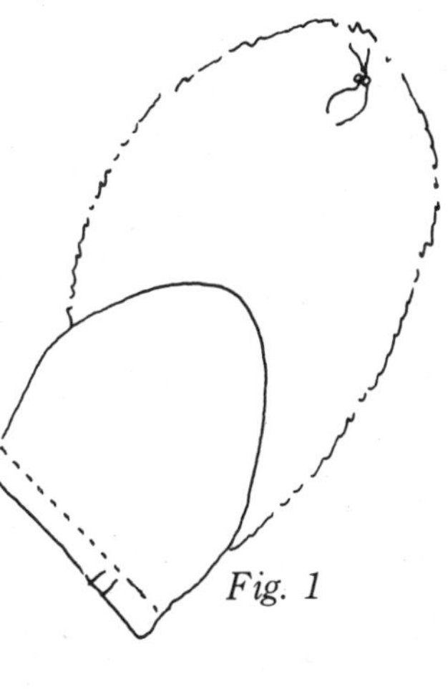

Fig. 1

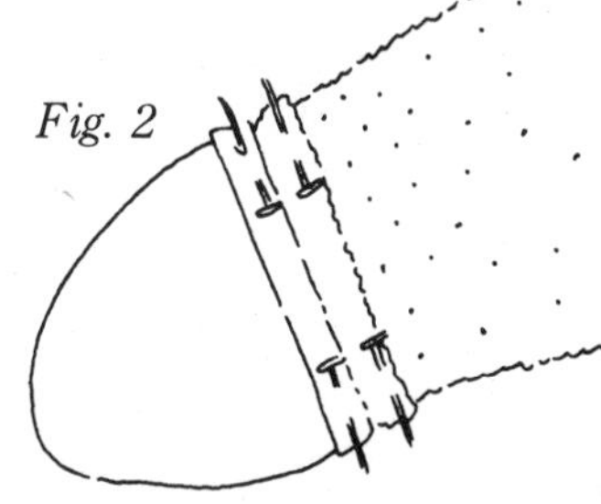

Fig. 2

3

Open out the paw and open the seam, pinning at each side so it remains open *(Fig. 2)*. Place the outer and inner arm pieces together, pile sides facing. Line them up, then pin them together at marks *A* and *B*. Continue pinning from *A* around the paw and up the other side of the arm. Make certain each notch is lined up with its matching notch. The outer arm is cut larger than the inner arm at the shoulder, so there will be loops of fabric between the notches that you will ease in during the sewing. When you are back at *B* and the arm is completely pinned *(Fig. 3)*, start stitching around the arm beginning at *A*. Again leave a ¼-inch seam allowance. When you reach the paw seam, see that the seam allowance is open when sewn down. Sew slowly, keeping the seams curved where they need to be. As you sew up the arm and around the shoulder, do not let any of the fabric travel and carefully ease it in between each notch.

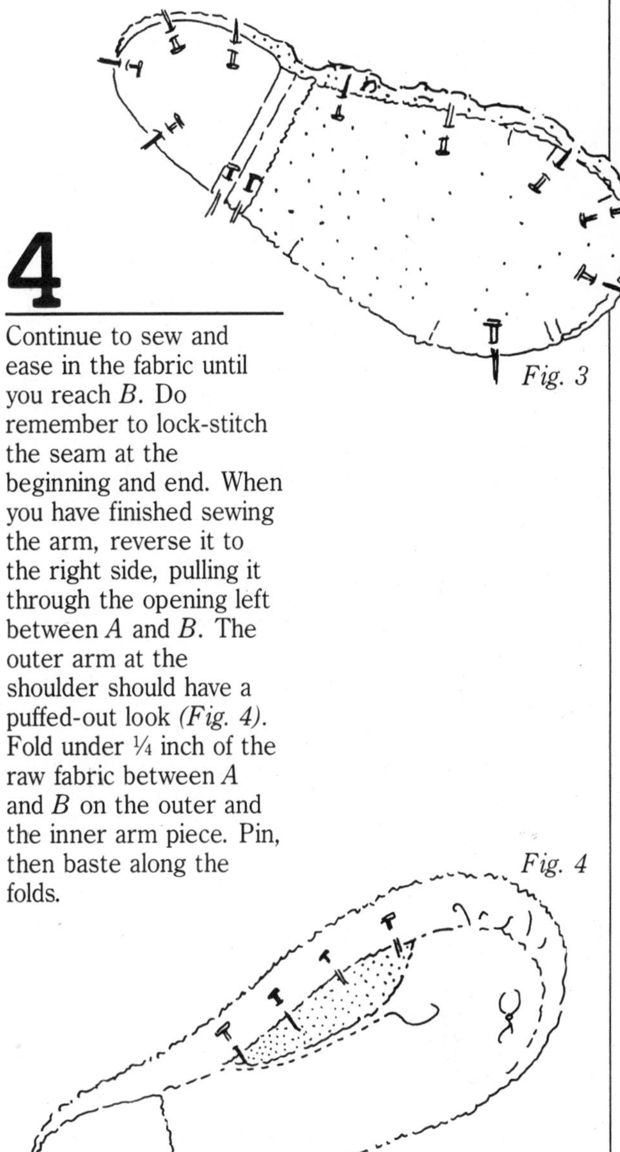

Fig. 3

4

Continue to sew and ease in the fabric until you reach *B*. Do remember to lock-stitch the seam at the beginning and end. When you have finished sewing the arm, reverse it to the right side, pulling it through the opening left between *A* and *B*. The outer arm at the shoulder should have a puffed-out look *(Fig. 4)*. Fold under ¼ inch of the raw fabric between *A* and *B* on the outer and the inner arm piece. Pin, then baste along the folds.

Fig. 4

5

Repeat steps 2 through 4 for the second arm. When the second arm is finished, put them both aside. Remember not to stitch closed the opening between *A* and *B* as it is through this opening that you will later insert the joint and stuff the arm.

THE LEGS

1

Each leg is constructed from 3 pieces: the fabric-covered cardboard pad, an outer and an inner leg. Place each leg's sections together, setting aside the pads for now.

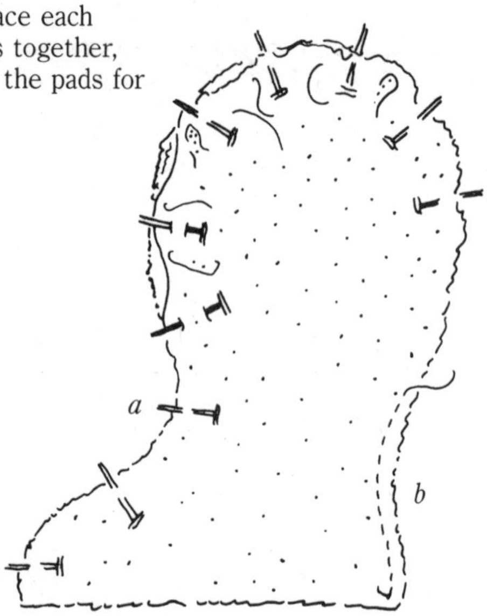

Fig. 1

2

On both inner leg pieces make a thread loop to mark where the joint will go. Working one leg at a time, place the 2 leg pieces together so that the pile of the outer leg faces the pile of the inner leg. Since the outer leg piece is larger, line the legs up at the bottoms, matching *B* and *F* of both pieces. Pin at these points first, and then continue to pin up both sides of the leg to the first set of notches on each side. From there on, match each pair of notches at the front and back of the leg and pin *(Fig. 1a)*. The excess fabric on the outer leg will have to be eased in during the sewing, just as you did with the arms.

3

When the leg is completely pinned, it is ready to be stitched. As usual, leave a ¼-inch seam allowance, lock-stitching at the beginning and end of the seam. Begin sewing at *B (Fig. 1b)* and sew up the leg, around the thigh and down the front of the leg and foot to *F*. Sew slowly and do not let the fabric travel. Carefully ease in the excess fullness. Leave open the bottom of the foot between *B* and *F*.

4

Turn the leg pile side out. There should be a puffed-out look at the top of the leg just as there is on the 2 arms. Fold under ¼ inch of the raw edge of the foot bottom. Pin, then baste close to the fold *(Fig. 2)*. Check that the loop mark is there for the joint.

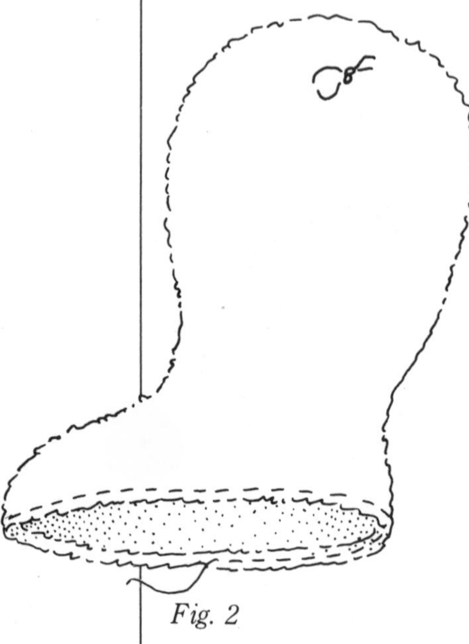

Fig. 2

5

Repeat steps 2 through 4 for the second leg. Set the pair of legs aside.

MAMA BEAR

A talented needle artist who has a passion for hats.

Mama wears her bonnet high in the back with the brim shading most of her face. When she is in profile, you can just see her nose peeking out from under.

Some picot-edged ribbon and material swatches used in making Mama's outfit.

If you wish, use arrangements of artificial flowers and leaves as part of the bonnet trim.

Mama's apron ties in a big bow at the back.

Mama measures 14 inches in height.

Mama's name is Berthe, as that was the name of her grandmother. She is a lighter shade of honey than Papa, which adds to her feminine qualities. Her Empire-styled apron, with its high waistline, is flattering to her somewhat ample figure, and the perky bonnet she wears is trimmed with ribbons and spring flowers. Mama loves needlework and included is her very latest needlepoint piece that you, too, may make.

Mama's Teddy Bear needlepoint can be mounted and framed after blocking.

REGISTERING A TEDDY BEAR

The important papers of all homemade Teddy Bears should include a registration certificate. Photocopy the one featured below for each bear you make. If giving a bear as a gift, include a copy of its certificate.

Official Teddy Bear Registration Certificate

Breed: Purebred Teddy Bear *Born:*

Sex: *Color(s):*

Registered Name:

Made By:

Owned By:

Owner's Address:

Certified by

Peggy Bialosky — *Peggy Bialosky*

Alan M. Bialosky — *Alan Bialosky*

Robert Tynes — *Robert Tynes*

ATTACHING THE LIMBS

You have now put together the head, body, two arms and two legs. Also on hand are the two finished foot pads. You are now ready to put the parts together. The arms and legs are to be joined to the body with crown joints. (Do *not* proceed if you have not practiced and mastered making a crown joint. Instead turn to page 19 for instructions.) It will be easier to start with the arms, since you can open out the body of the bear and easily see inside.

1

Lay the body pile side out on your work surface. The front opening should be facing up. Open out the body at the neck so you can see inside to the arm joint marks. Place the arms on each side of the body, making sure the right arm is on the right side of the body and the left one is on the left side. A quick way to double-check is to see that the arm openings are to the back. Also, the upper arm fullness should be on the outside of the arm and away from the body. The 2 thread loops on the arm and body should be facing each other. When you have the arms correctly placed, set one arm aside, leaving the one you plan on joining to the body first.

An inside view of correctly made crown joints which attach the limbs to the bear's body.

2

Take a joint set: 2 wood or hardboard discs (also known as hardboard washers), 2 small metal washers, and 1 cotter pin. Onto the cotter pin first slip a small metal washer, next one of the large wood or hardboard discs. Put this aside. Open the arm to the inside, and with your awl very carefully push a hole through the joint mark on the fabric. Work from the inside of the arm and push the point of the awl through to the outside. Make the hole only as large as the thickness of the cotter pin. Work slowly so as not to rip the fabric.

3

When the hole is the correct size, remove the awl and take the cotter pin with the disc and washer and slip the point of the cotter pin into the hole from the inside of the arm. Pull the pin all the way through so that the disc is pressing against the inside of the arm fabric. Lay this aside for a moment.

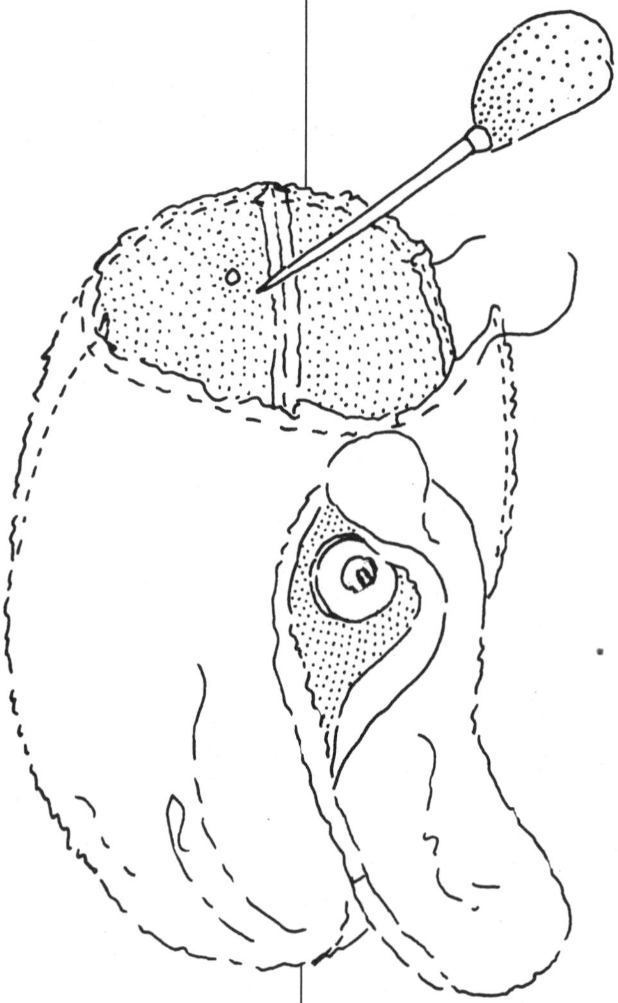

4

Take your awl, and from the inside of the body, push the awl through the arm mark on the body until you have the size hole you need. Remove the awl and push the tip of the cotter pin through the hole from the outside of the body to the inside. Your thread loop will help you to locate the hole on the right side of the fabric. When the cotter pin is completely through, slip the second large disc and then the small metal washer onto the pin on the body side. Remove the thread loops. You are now ready to form the crown of the joint (see page 22, if necessary).

5

When you have completed joining the first arm, continue on to the second and proceed in the same way. When the arms have been attached, you are ready for the legs.

6

Just as you have done with the arms, place the right leg to the right side of the body and the left leg to the left side. Decide which leg you will work on first and set the other one aside. Place the metal washer and disc on the cotter pin and set aside. Since you will be working through the foot of the bear leg, pull the upper part of the leg down through the leg until you can see the mark made on the inside of the fabric for the joint. Use your awl to carefully make the hole necessary for the cotter pin. While the leg is still partially pulled through the bottom of the foot and the joint hole is showing, slip the cotter pin (with the washer and disc) into the hole and out to the right side of the leg. Holding on to the tip of the pin, pull the fabric out of the leg so that the leg is once again lying flat and the pile is on the outside.

7

Make the leg joint hole on the body, again working the awl from the inside of the body to the outside. Push the cotter pin tip through the hole from the right side of the body to the inside. Slip on the disc and washer and you are ready to form the crown joint. Cut away marking loops. Repeat for the second leg.

STUFFING THE BEARS

When your crown joints are completed and both legs and both arms have been joined to the body, you are ready to begin stuffing the bear's body. Before you begin, keep in mind that the stuffing must be firm, not lumpy, and—important—see that you pack the stuffing all around the crown joints.

THE BODY

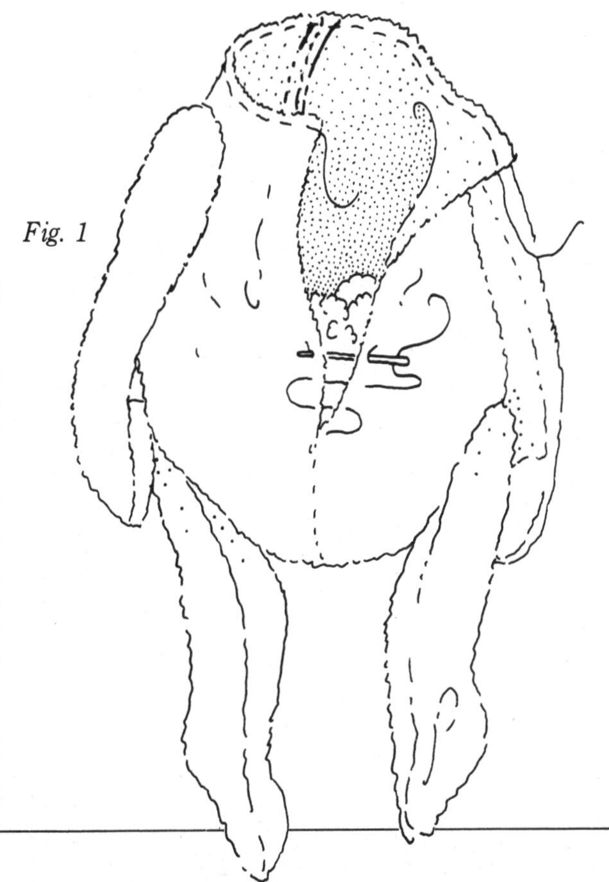

Fig. 1

1

To begin, open out the upper part of the body, and taking a small handful of stuffing material, press it into the crotch area. Continue to firmly stuff, working up from the crotch and leg joint area until you have stuffed well past the joints. When you are past the bottom of the front opening, it is time to start sewing up the front.

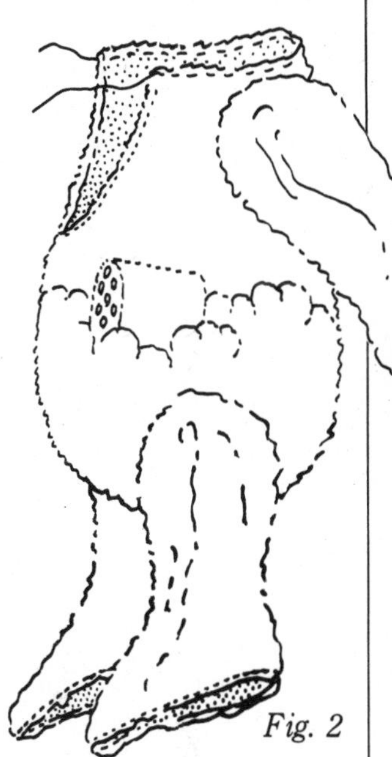

Fig. 2

2

Wax a long strand of carpet thread with beeswax. Use it doubled and be sure to knot the end. At the very bottom of the opening *X* mark, run the threaded needle from the inside to the outside, pulling the thread all the way out. With 2 fingers, press together the 2 folded edges of the center opening near the bottom and *X* mark. Ladder-stitch the 2 sides together, using small stitches and working close to the folded edge *(Fig. 1)*. When you have sewn it about halfway up and have reached the stomach area, if you wish to put in a voice box, now is the time. Before you place the voice box into the body, check and see if you have stuffed the bottom half of the body firmly enough. If need be, add more stuffing, leaving a well in the middle for the voice box. When the body is firm enough, place the voice box into the well. The voice box is a cylinder and one end is covered with small round holes; be sure that this end faces toward the front and is close to the stomach fabric *(Fig 2)*.

3

When the cylinder is in place, continue to stuff the body. Be careful not to let the voice box travel to the back or upward in the body. Ease a thin, smooth layer of stuffing in front of the cylinder so that the rounded outline does not show through the bear's stomach. Be careful not to use too much stuffing, though, as it will mute the "growl." Continue to stuff and stitch until you reach the neck. Once you have reached the neck, lock the seam and clip the excess thread. Check to see that you have not caught the gathering thread running around the neckline in the front stitching.

4

Pull the neckline thread slightly to tighten that seam, but not so tightly as to cause the fabric to gather. Tie off and push the ends into the body. If necessary, add more stuffing so the entire body and neck section is nice and firm but not hard. You want a bear, not a rock, to cuddle. Set the bear on your work surface so that it is lying on its back, and you will now be ready to start stuffing the legs.

THE LEGS

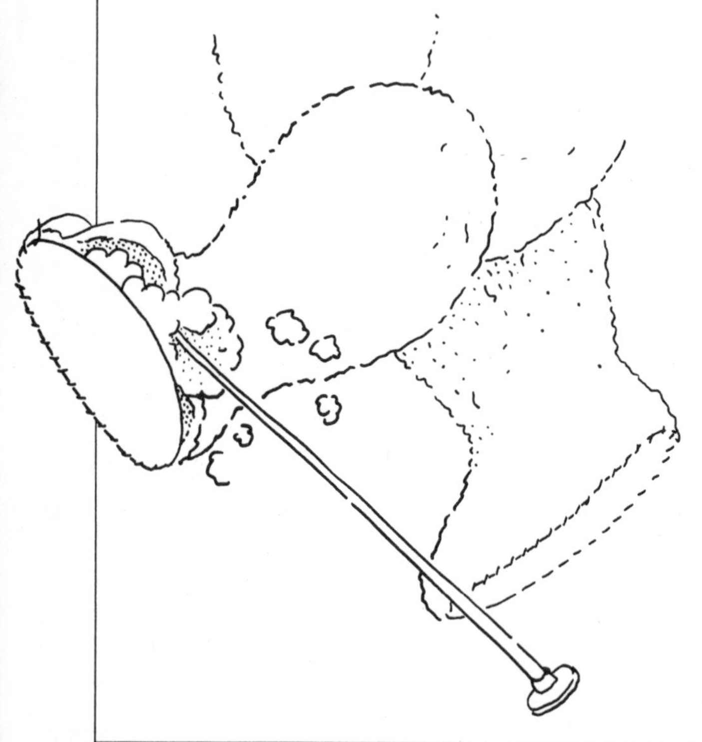

1

Take a small handful of stuffing and begin to ease it through the opening at the bottom of the foot and up into one of the legs. Work it all the way up into the rounded thigh area. If you cannot reach that far into the leg with your fingers, use a knitting needle to work the stuffing all the way up. Continue stuffing, making certain that the leg is well packed and the joint is completely surrounded by your stuffing material. As you work down the leg, mold it slightly if necessary to keep it rounded and unlumpy. Work slowly and carefully since the stuffing will influence how your bear will look and move. By the time you have the leg half filled you will know if your crown joint has been done tightly enough. Just move the leg to a position you want. If it holds that position, the crown joint is right and everything is fine. If not, the joint is too loose. At this stage, if it is too loose, it will be up to you to decide if you want to undo everything and redo the joints. Alas, it is only at this point that one can tell for certain if the joints were made tight enough.

2

When you have reached the foot area and have partly stuffed it, you are ready to begin sewing on the foot pad. Make certain that you have the correct foot pad for the leg you are working on, since there is a right and a left one. Line up the center line, which is marked *(F)* and drawn on the card side of the pad, with the front seam line of the leg. Pin straight through the basted edge of the foot fabric and into the edge of the fabric-covered card. Line up *B* and the center line with the back leg seam and run another pin through the edge of the basted fabric at the foot and into the side of the card.

3

Wax a length of thread with beeswax. Using it doubled, slip-stitch the foot pad and leg together starting at *B* and working around one side to *F*. Use a small slip stitch, catching the foot fabric along the folded edge and the edge of the pad fabric that rolls over the card edge. When the pad and leg have been stitched as far as *F*, begin to pack in more stuffing, to shape the sewn side of the foot.

4

Continue to stitch to about halfway along the unsewn side, then work stuffing into the toe area of the foot. Stuff firmly, working the stuffing into the heel also. Before completely sewing the opening closed, check the foot once more and if necessary add more stuffing, using the knitting needle to work it through the opening. Finish sewing and lock-stitch, but before you clip the thread, run the needle up into the leg away from the foot. Bring the needle out of the fabric, pull and then clip the thread.

5

For the second leg, repeat steps 1 through 4. Stuffing something well is not easy and it takes time. Also, you will be very surprised just how much stuffing it can take to do the job.

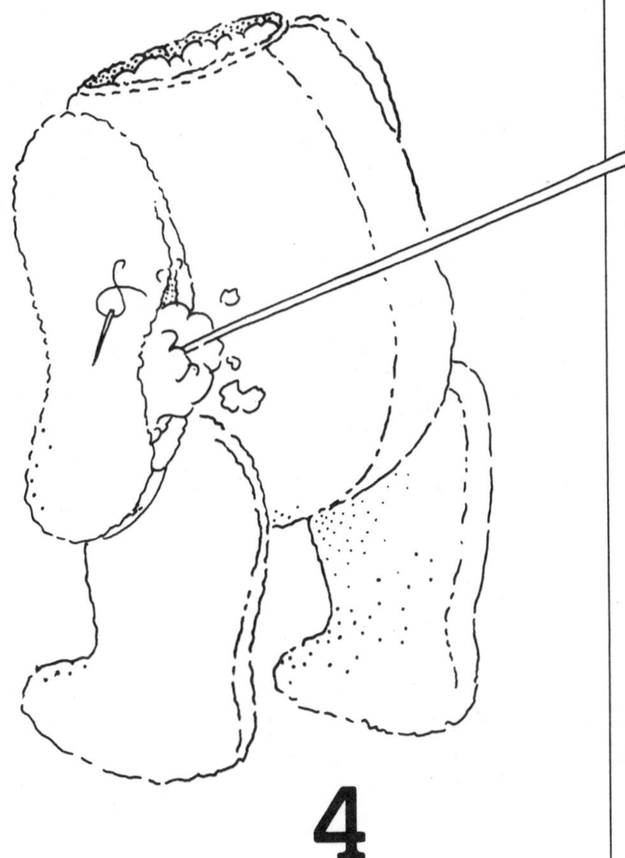

THE ARMS

1

To stuff the arms, first turn your bear over onto its stomach so that the arm seam openings are facing up.

2

Stuff each arm as carefully as you have already done the legs. Begin by stuffing from the upper part of the arm to the seam opening. Then stuff the paw end up to the seam opening. When the 2 ends of the arm are nice and firm, not lumpy, begin to work stuffing into the middle section of the arm. Work the stuffing toward the front of the arm first, and then fill in the back part.

3

When this section of the arm feels firm, wax a length of carpet thread. Using it doubled, begin closing up the seam. Use a small ladder stitch, catching both layers of the folded edge of each side. When you have the opening about half closed, add more stuffing if needed. Continue to sew, adding more stuffing as you go, until the seam is completely closed. End the seam and lock-stitch, then run the needle into the arm, away from the seam. Bring the needle out, pull the thread and clip.

4

Repeat steps 1 through 3 for the second arm. When the arm is complete, you are ready to begin the head.

THE HEAD

1

Turn the head upside down so that the neck opening is facing up. Taking a small handful of stuffing, work it into the nose. Really take care that you force it well into the end of the nose. This section is thick and stiff with seams and embroidery stitching, and if you do not check carefully, you will find you have a bear with a floppy, weak nose. Continue to pack the stuffing into this area until it is filled and you have begun to fill the chin area.

Fig. 1

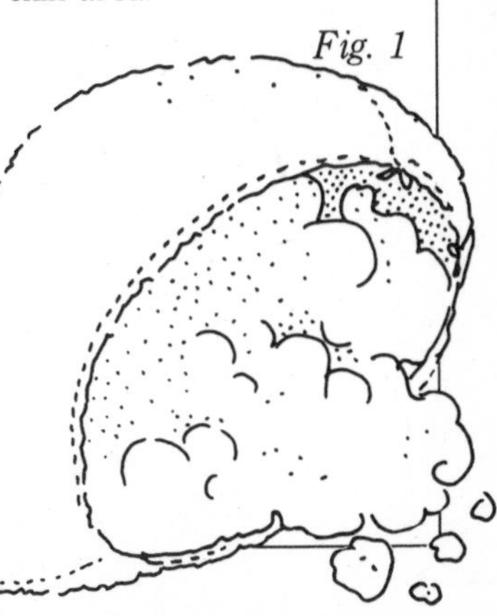

2

Start filling the top and back of the head. Now you'll have to stuff everywhere at the same time. If you work too much in one area it will cause the head to start to lose its true shape. Continue to stuff, packing in your stuffing until the entire head is firm and the seams do not pucker. Mold the head between your hands, keeping it in a rounded shape with a good pointed muzzle. The embroidered nose should be centered at the end of the muzzle.

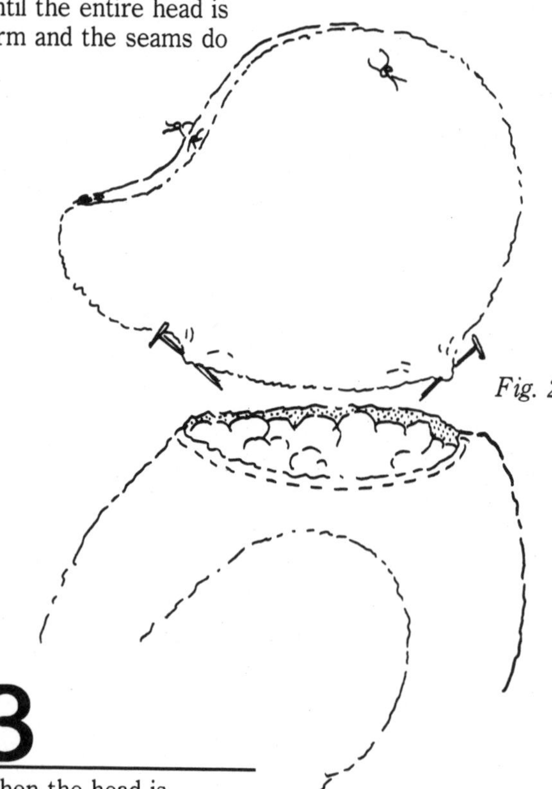

Fig. 2

3

When the head is completely stuffed, sit the bear's body in front of you, with its back facing you. Take a T-pin and push it into the fold of fabric on the head at the neck mark *D* (you have stitched a loop of thread there as a marker). See that the T-pin is on an angle so that the point will come out through the neck, near the folded fabric *(Fig. 2)*.

4

Place the head on the neck of the body so that the T-pin is lined up with the center back seam of the body at *D*. Push the T-pin down through the head and into the folded neck fabric of the body at *D*. Push another T-pin through the folded neck fabric of the head at the front center seam *A* and push it into the neck fabric of the body at *A*.

5

Continue to pin the head to the body, first working along one side and then the other, easing it together if necessary. If you want your bear to face front when finished, you must make certain that the front and back seams—*A* and *D* of head and body—are perfectly aligned and remain that way throughout the pinning and sewing. If you wish your bear to look to one side, let the head seams *A* and *D* slip past body seams *A* and *D (Fig. 3)*. *Note:* Mama bear in this book was made so that her head looks slightly to one side.

Fig. 3

6

When you are ready to start sewing, wax a long strand of carpet thread with beeswax. You will be using it doubled. Knot the thread, and starting from the inside at center back *D*, push the needle through to the right side and begin to whip-stitch the head to the body, using small stitches. Continue to sew the two parts together, removing the T-pins as you go. Continue to sew past the center front *A* seams and around the second side until the head and body are about three-quarters joined. Remove the remaining T-pins, and with your finger or a knitting needle, force more stuffing through the remaining opening. Push the stuffing up close to the neck seams and continue to stuff so that the head is firm and not wobbly on the body. Finish sewing the head to the body, adding more stuffing if needed.

7

Finish where you began, at center back *D*. Lock the seam, then push the needle and thread through the last stitch and into the chest, bringing the needle out an inch or two from the actual seam. Pull the thread and clip.

DESIGNING THE FACE

THE MOUTH

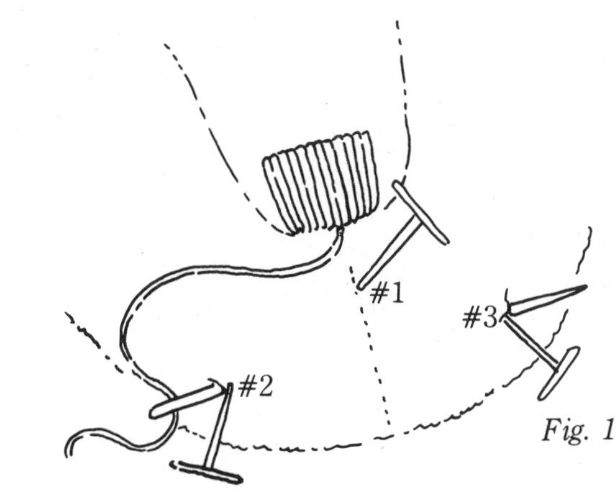

Fig. 1

1

Measure down from the bottom of the nose, on the center face seam, about ½ inch to ¾ inch. Place a T-pin at an angle *(Fig. 1, #1)*. Sink the pin well into the head. Sink a second T-pin about 1½ inches away from the center seam and about ½ lower than pin #1 *(Fig. 1, #2)*. Place a third T-pin the same distance from the center seam on the opposite side of the head and parallel to pin #2.

2

Slip the end of the black embroidery thread that has been left hanging loose at the bottom of the nose onto a long needle.

3

Push the threaded needle into the fabric at the base of T-pin #2. Push it through the fabric and stuffing to the other side, bringing it out at the base of pin #3. Remove both pins.

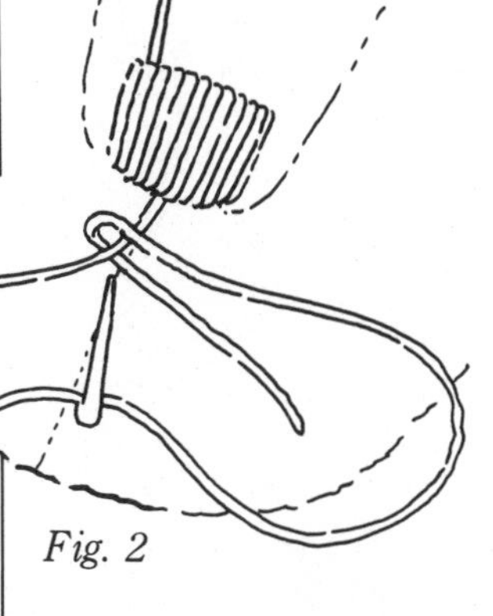
Fig. 2

4

Pull the embroidery thread until most of the extra thread between the bottom of the nose and #2 has been pulled through the head and out at #3, leaving only a small loop of thread. Run your needle *under* the loop, then bring it up and over the loop and push the needle down into the fabric at #1 *(Fig. 2)*. Push the needle through the fabric, bringing it out at the top edge of the nose embroidery. Pull the thread until the mouth stitches are tight enough to lie flat on the surface of the fabric *(Fig. 3)*. Remove pin #1.

Fig. 3

5

Push the needle back down into the nose stitching at the top edge of the nose, and bring the needle out at the bottom of the nose *(Fig. 3)*. Repeat this stitching 2 or 3 more times and then clip the thread close to the nose. By doing this there will be no knots showing and the mouth stitching will be secure. The mouth is finished.

Note: By placing the T-pins in slightly different positions, you can form all manner of mouth shapes. Before you start to actually sew, try several different pin positions. Hold the embroidery thread at pin #2, bring it up to #1, looping it over that pin and down to pin #3. This should give you a good idea of how the expression will turn out.

THE EYES

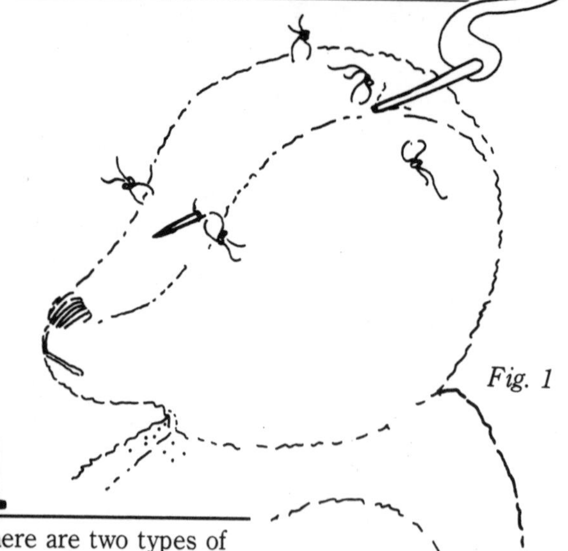

Fig. 1

1

There are two types of glass eyes. If you have chosen the kind with the preformed loops, you will be ready to proceed. If you have the wire shank kind, follow the illustrated instructions for forming the loops on page 11 before proceeding with step 2.

2

Wax a length of medium-weight cotton string with beeswax. Thread a 12-inch toymaker's needle with a double length of the string. Ease the point of the needle into the center section of the head near the inside of the ear mark. Push the needle at an angle so that it passes through the head and comes out where the eye mark is *(Fig. 1)*.

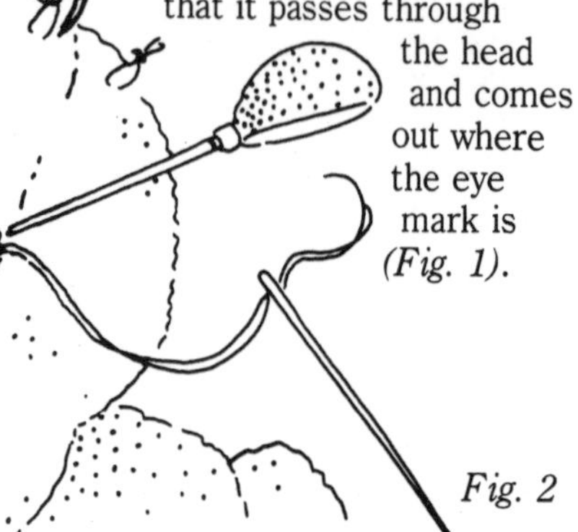

Fig. 2

3

Pull the needle and string out of the head at the eye mark, until about 4 or 5 inches of string remain at the ear mark. Force your awl into the eye mark just beside the string, and loosen the fabric and stuffing until you have a small hole about the size of the eye loop *(Fig. 2)*. Remove the eye-marking loop.

4

Run your needle through the loop of one eye and return the point of the needle to the enlarged eye opening. Again, push the needle at an angle and bring it out near the inside of the ear mark on the side section of the head *(Fig. 3)*.

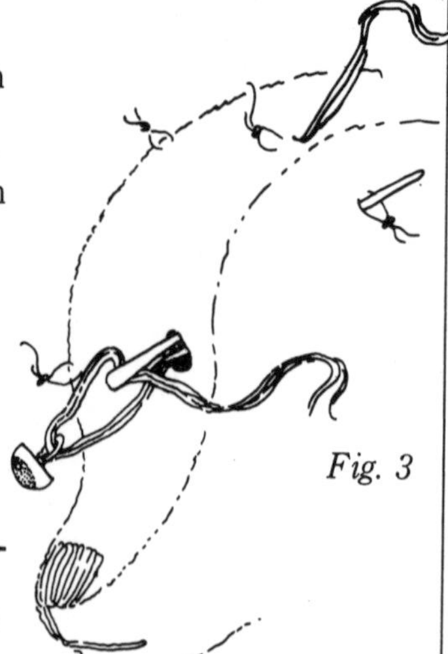

Fig. 3

5

Pull the needle out from the ear mark and tighten the string until the eye loop is tight against the fabric. Using your awl, stretch open the fabric until you are able to slip the eye's loop through and into the stuffing. Be patient (and careful), as this takes a little doing.

6

When the loop has slipped into the head, remove the needle. Pull both ends of the string tight and make a single tie in the string, tying all 4 string ends. Continue pulling and tightening the string until the eye is tightly embedded in the head and not at all loose. The wire loop should not show at all and the base of the eye should press flat against the head. When it is correctly done, the tension formed by the tied string and the eye will form a well, or eye socket, around the eye itself.

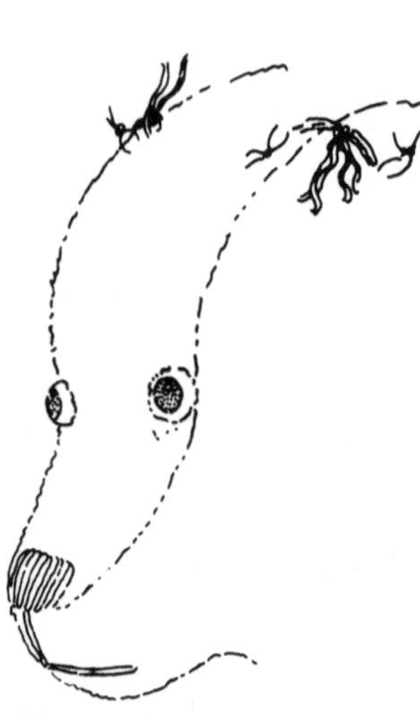

Fig. 4

7

When the eye is correctly set, tie off the string several more times so that the knot is secure. Leave about an inch of string at the end of the knot and clip the rest.

8

Repeat steps 2 through 7 for the second eye. With the eyes in place you have a bear face to look at, at last.
If you prefer, you can embroider the eyes, using a satin stitch, or securely attach circles of felt with slip stitching.

THE EARS

1

Check to see that the 4 ear pieces are correctly matched into pairs. With pile sides facing, stitch each pair together, leaving a ¼-inch seam allowance, around the curve from *A* to *B*. Leave the bottoms open. Lock-stitch the seam at both ends.

2

Turn the ears right side out. Fold under and pin ¼ inch of the raw bottom edge of each ear and baste it in place *(Fig. 1)*. Set aside one ear and proceed with the other.

3

Push a T-pin into the basted edge of the ear front at a corner. Pin the front over the ear mark on the center section of the head *(Fig. 2, #1)*. Use another T-pin to secure the other tip of the ear (#2) to the mark at the side section of the head. Next, push the knotted eye strings into the ear itself.

4

Insert a third T-pin into the front of the ear where it crosses the head seam (#3).

5

Insert a fourth T-pin into the bottom edge at the back of the ear, just to the side of the seam (#4). Pull the back part of the ear to the back of the head and pin in place. When the ear is pinned, the shape at the base of the ear should be similar to a crescent moon. The ear is now ready to be sewn, since it doesn't require stuffing.

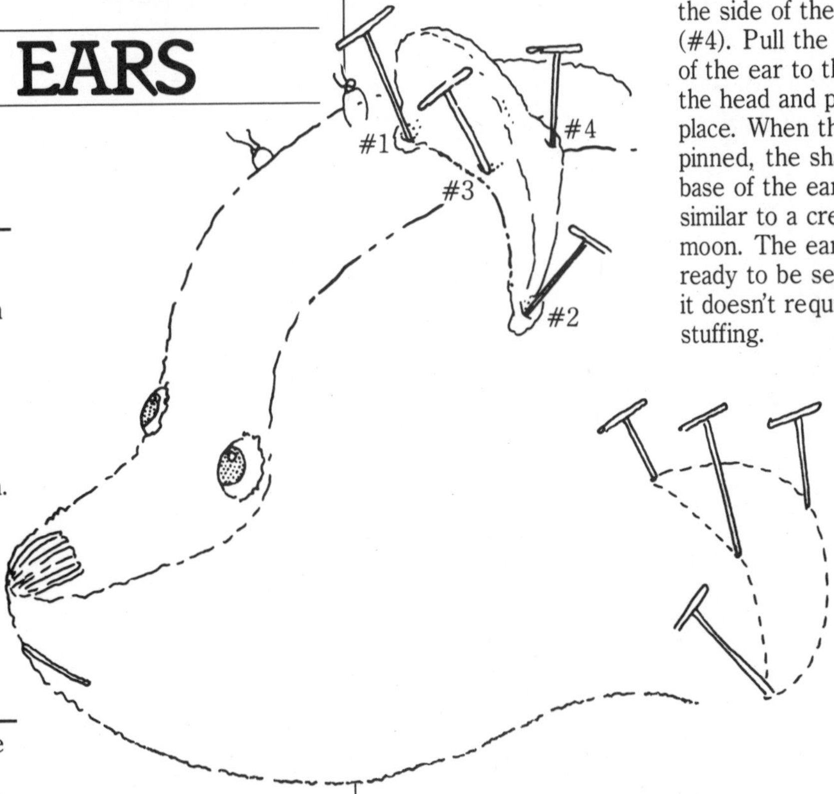

Fig. 2

6

Wax a length of carpet thread. Double the thread. Slip-stitch the ear to the head, using small stitches. When it is completely sewn in place, run the threaded needle back and forth from one side of the ear to the other several times, where the ear joins the head. This will secure the stitching. When finished, clip the thread.

7

Repeat steps 3 through 6 for the second ear.

Congratulations, your bear is now finished!

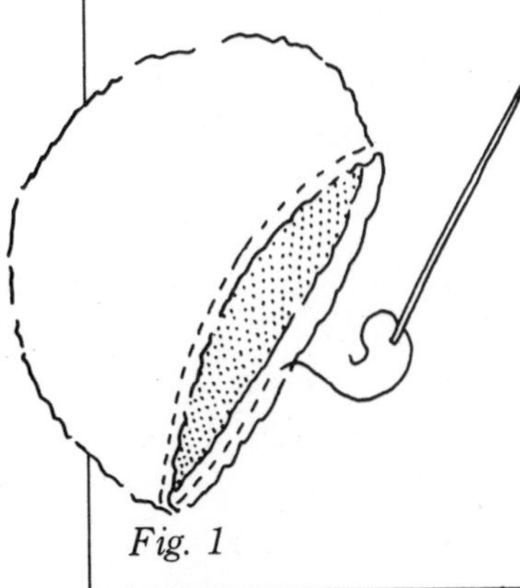

Fig. 1

PAPA BEAR

It is perhaps easiest to start by assembling Papa since he is the largest and therefore the easiest to work with. His finished height is approximately 17 inches. The pattern is the exact size and includes the seam allowances. You will not have to clip any of the seams or curves using this little amount of seam allowance.

MATERIALS NEEDED

Fur fabric for bear: 14 x 56 inches
Fabric for pads and paws: 8 × 10 inches
2 bags stuffing, each 16 oz. (Papa will need 1¾ bags)
2 pair (4) joints
1 pair glass eyes, 16 mm diameter
Voice box (optional)
Beeswax
Long-nosed pliers
Awl
T-pins
Straight pins
12-inch toymaker's needle
Tapestry needle, size 18/22
Sewing needles, various lengths
1 skein black embroidery thread or silk twist
4 feet medium-weight cotton string
Large spool of heavy-duty button thread to match
Large spool of mercerized thread to match

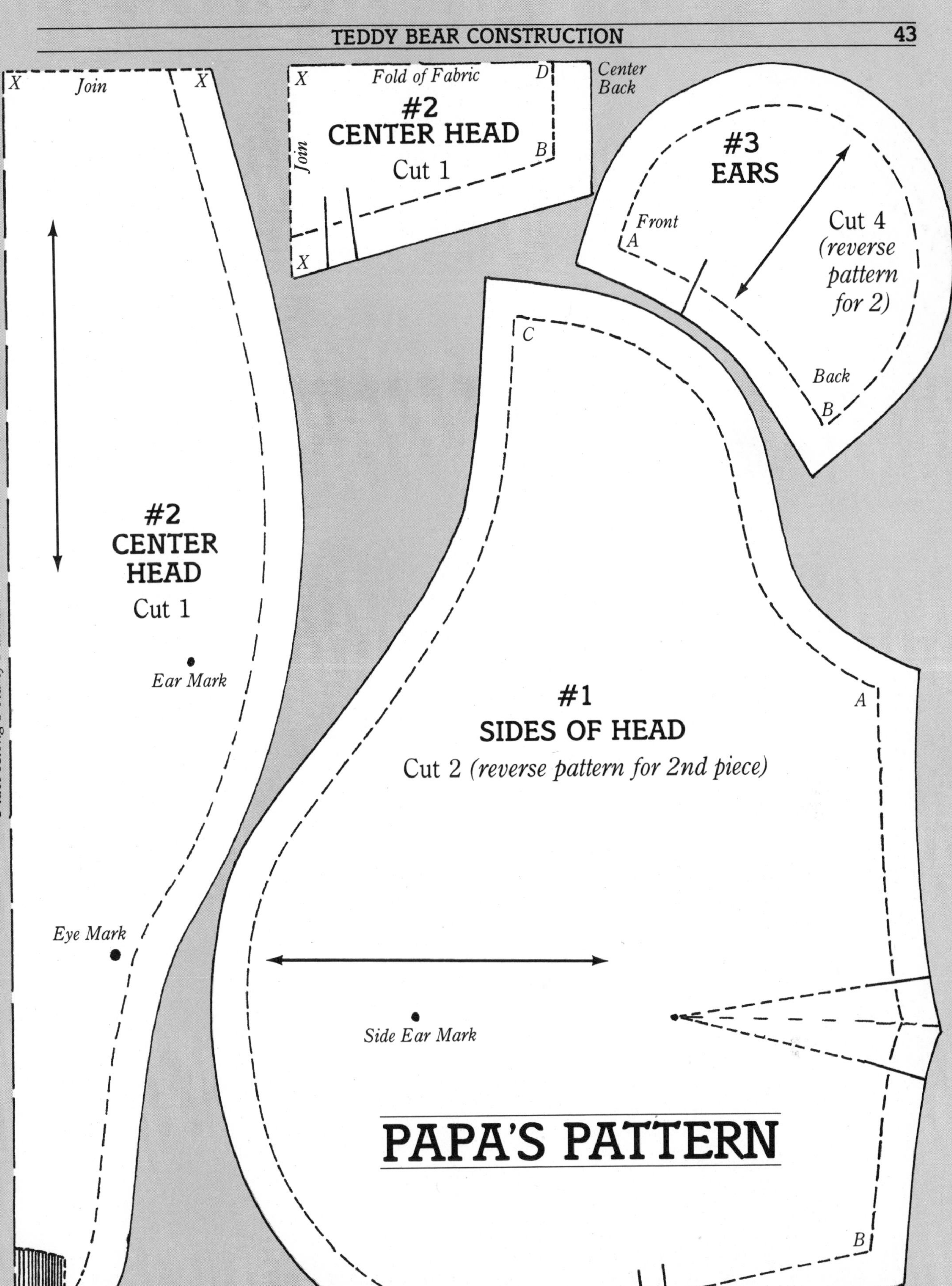
X
Join
X
#2
CENTER HEAD
Cut 1
Ear Mark
Eye Mark
C
Nose Tip Mark
X
Fold of Fabric
D
Center Back
#2
CENTER HEAD
Join
B
Cut 1
X
#3
EARS
Front
A
Cut 4 (reverse pattern for 2)
Back
B
C
#1
SIDES OF HEAD
Cut 2 (reverse pattern for 2nd piece)
A
Side Ear Mark
B
PAPA'S PATTERN

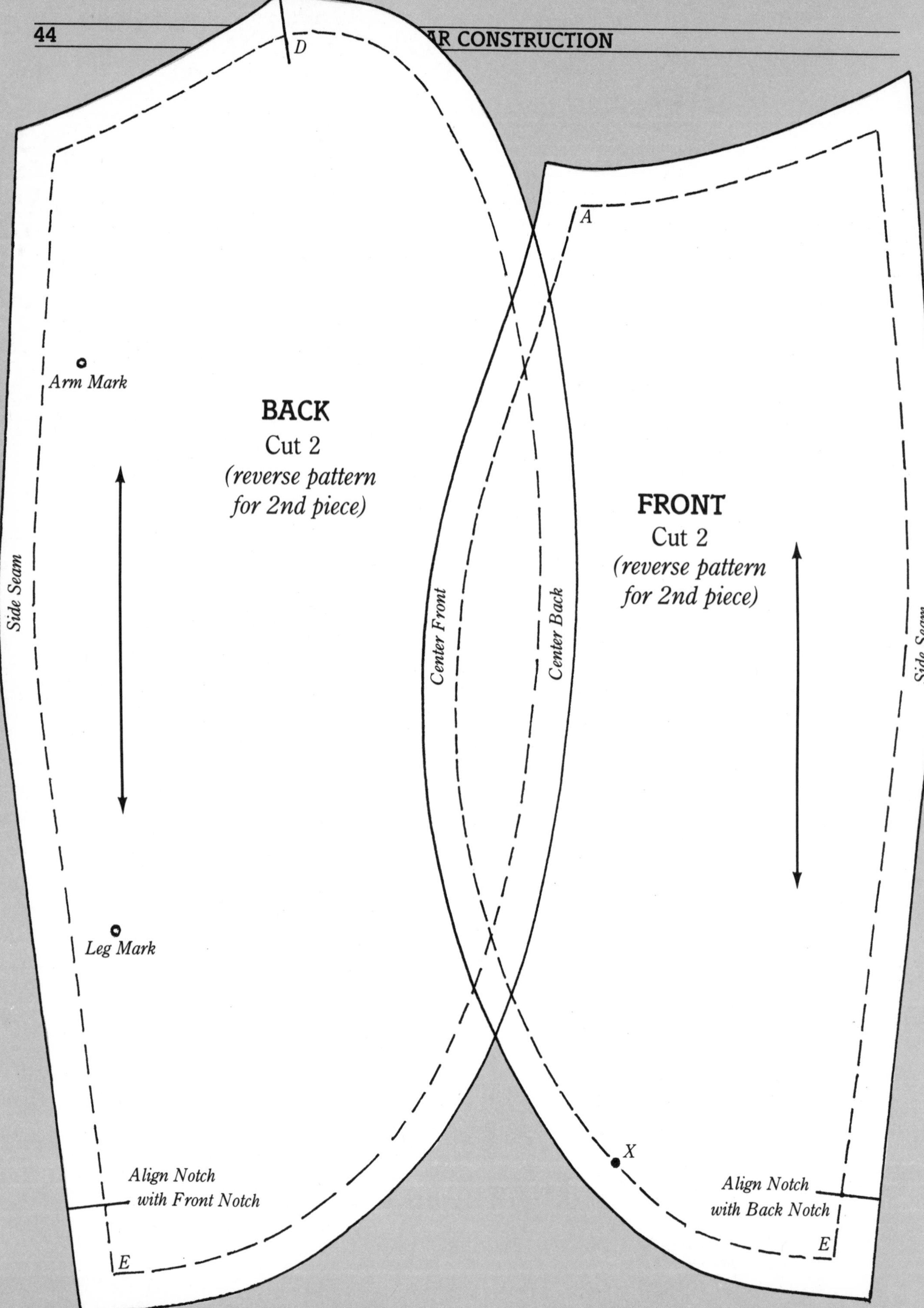
D
Arm Mark
BACK
Cut 2
(reverse pattern
for 2nd piece)
Side Seam
Leg Mark
Align Notch
with Front Notch
E
Center Front
Center Back
A
FRONT
Cut 2
(reverse pattern
for 2nd piece)
Side Seam
X
Align Notch
with Back Notch
E

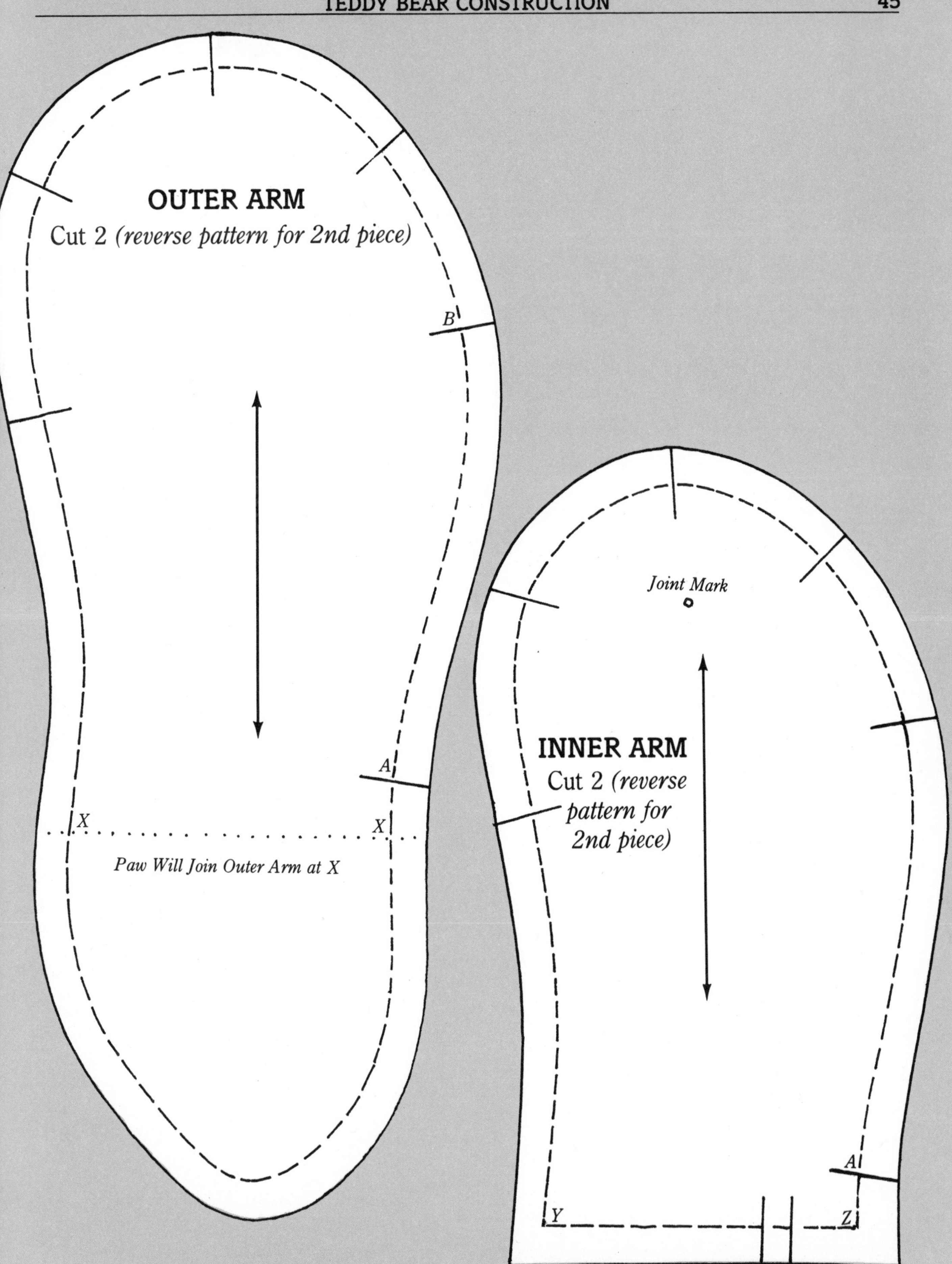
OUTER ARM
Cut 2 (reverse pattern for 2nd piece)
B
A
X
X
Paw Will Join Outer Arm at X
Joint Mark
INNER ARM
Cut 2 (reverse pattern for 2nd piece)
A
Y
Z

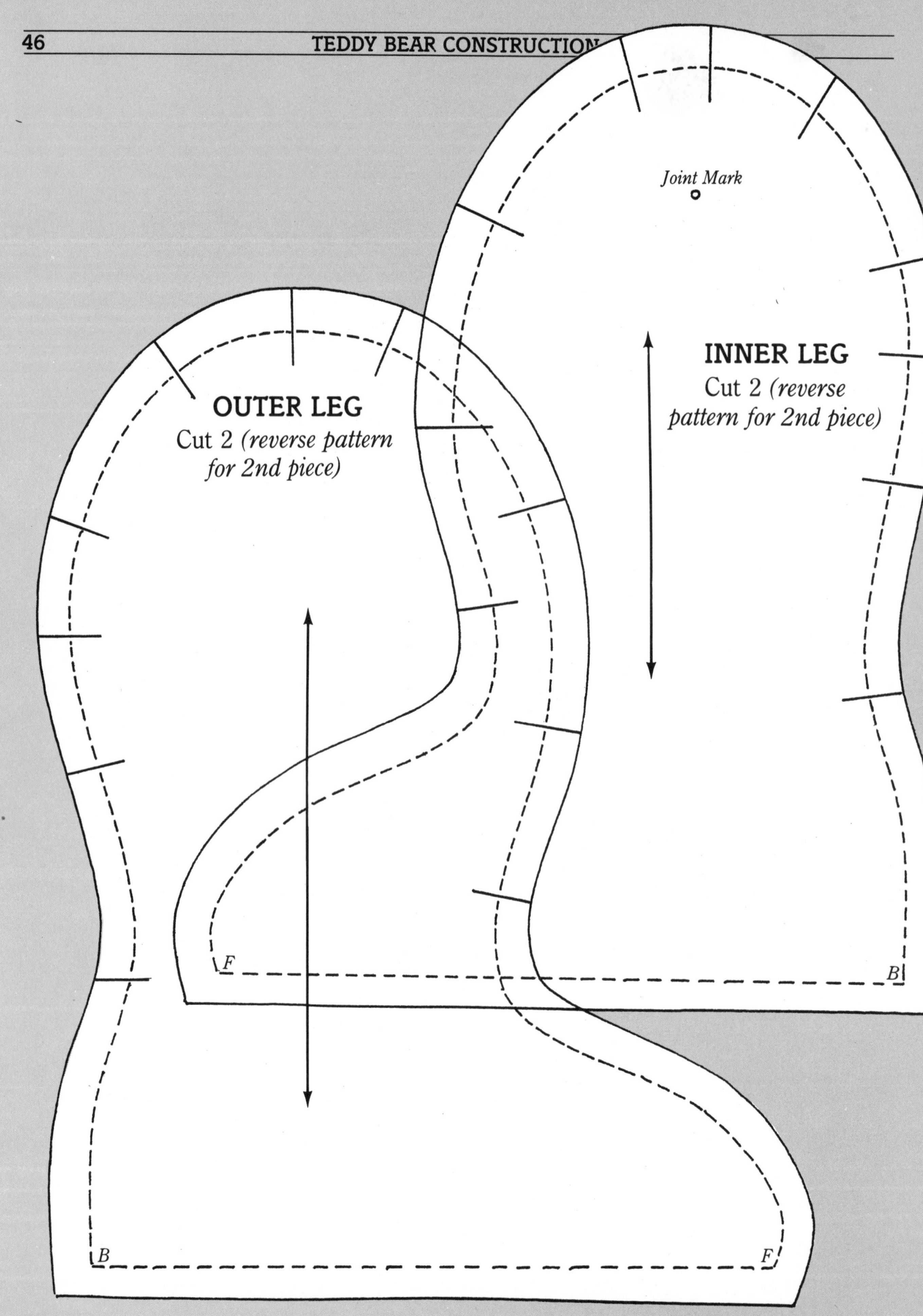
Joint Mark
INNER LEG
Cut 2 (reverse pattern for 2nd piece)
OUTER LEG
Cut 2 (reverse pattern for 2nd piece)
F
B
B
F

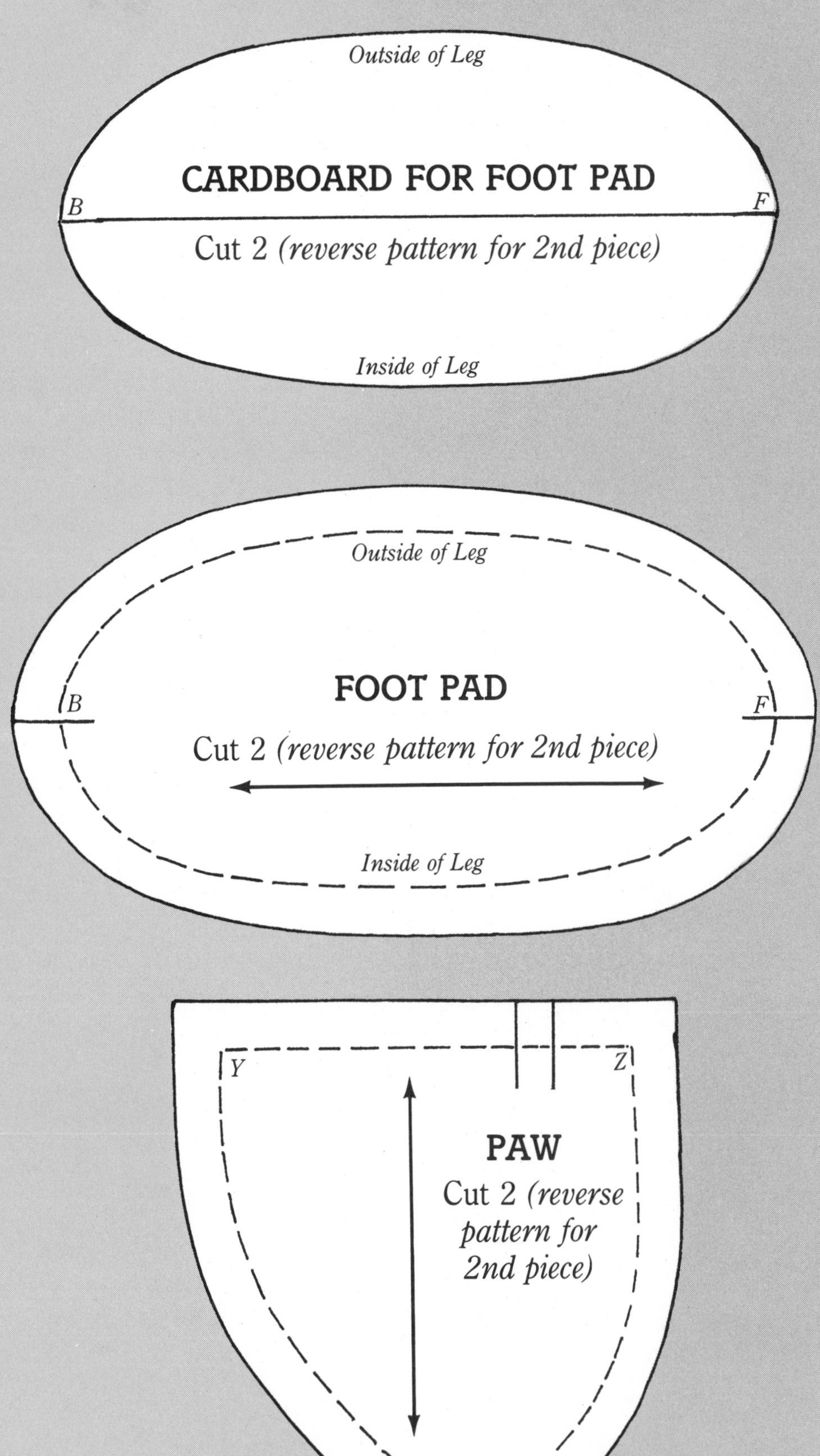
Outside of Leg
CARDBOARD FOR FOOT PAD
B
F
Cut 2 (reverse pattern for 2nd piece)
Inside of Leg
Outside of Leg
FOOT PAD
B
F
Cut 2 (reverse pattern for 2nd piece)
Inside of Leg
Y
Z
PAW
Cut 2 (reverse pattern for 2nd piece)

MAMA BEAR

When completed, Mama's height will measure approximately 14 inches. You will note that her head was attached so that she looks to one side (see step 5, page 38).

MATERIALS NEEDED

The materials needed are the same as those for Papa (see page 42) with only the following changes:

Fur fabric for bear: 13 x 43 inches

Fabric for pads and paws: 7 x 8 inches

2 bags stuffing, each 16 oz. (Mama will need 1½ bags)

1 pair glass eyes, 14 mm

MAMA'S PATTERN

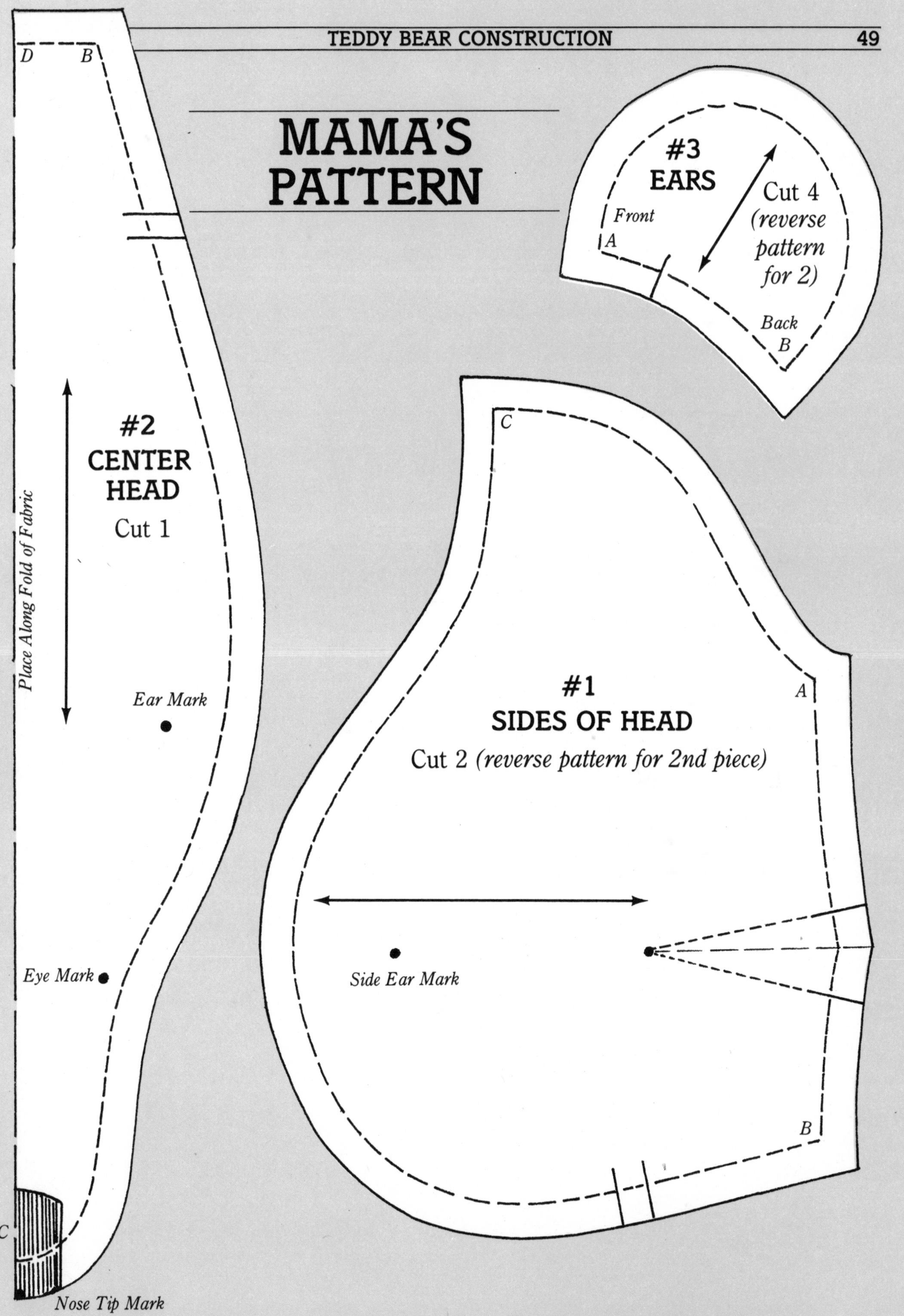

D

Arm Mark

BACK

Cut 2 *(reverse pattern for 2nd piece)*

Side Seam

Center Back

Leg Mark

Align Notch with Front Notch

E

A

FRONT

Cut 2 *(reverse pattern for 2nd piece)*

Center Front

Side Seam

X

Align Notch with Back Notch

E

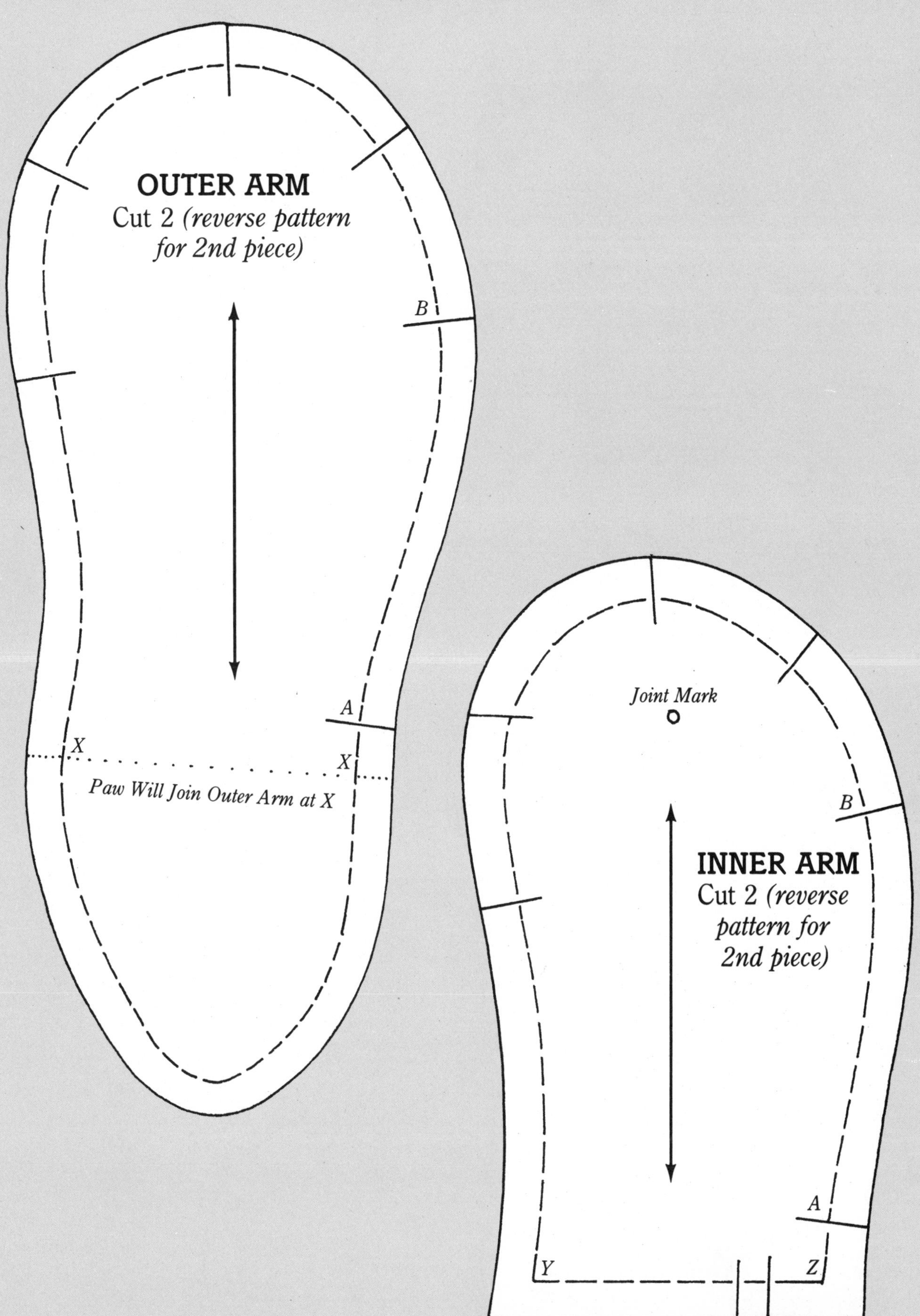
OUTER ARM
Cut 2 (reverse pattern for 2nd piece)
B
A
X
X
Paw Will Join Outer Arm at X
Joint Mark
B
INNER ARM
Cut 2 (reverse pattern for 2nd piece)
A
Y
Z

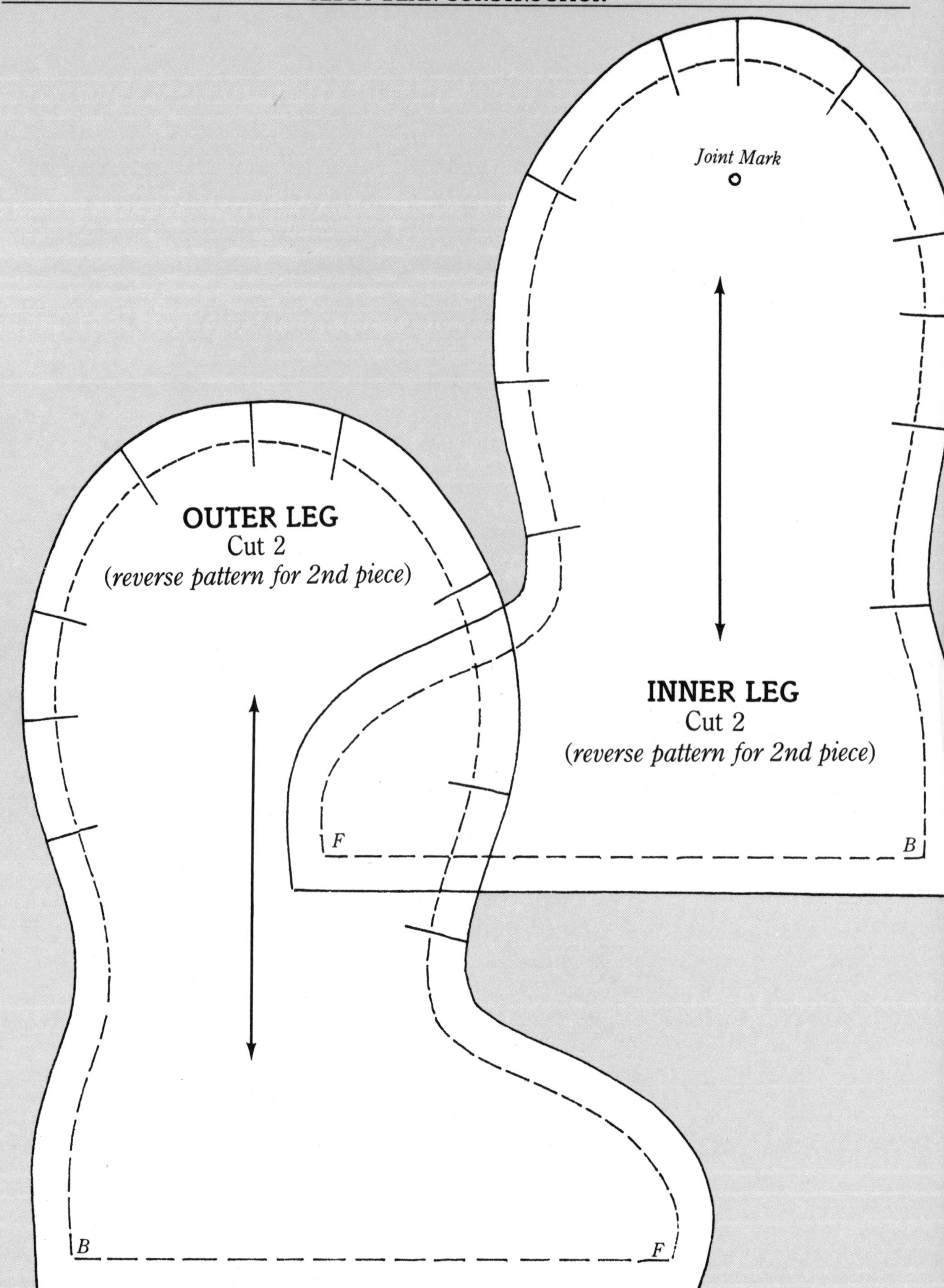
Joint Mark
INNER LEG
Cut 2
(reverse pattern for 2nd piece)
F
B
OUTER LEG
Cut 2
(reverse pattern for 2nd piece)
B
F

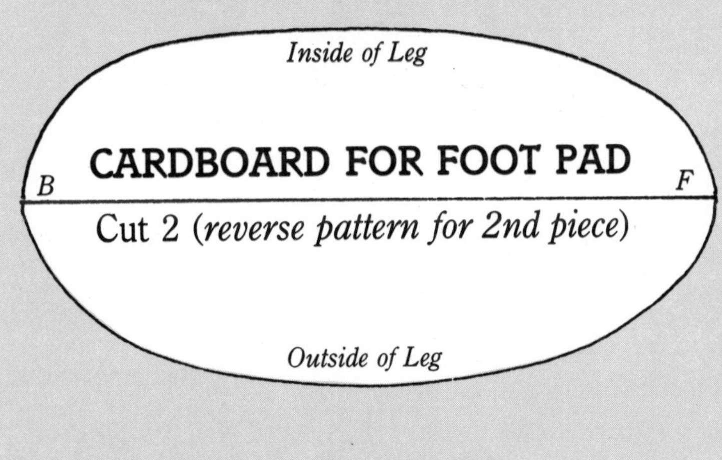
Inside of Leg
CARDBOARD FOR FOOT PAD
B
F
Cut 2 (*reverse pattern for 2nd piece*)
Outside of Leg

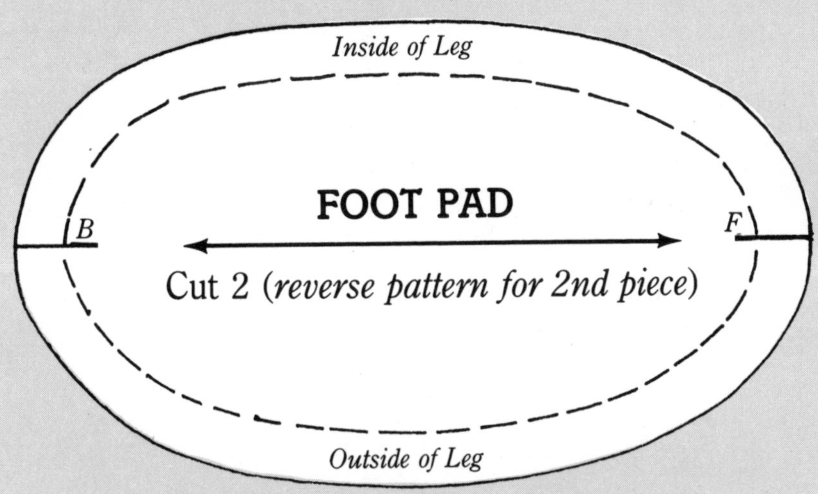
Inside of Leg
FOOT PAD
B
F
Cut 2 (*reverse pattern for 2nd piece*)
Outside of Leg

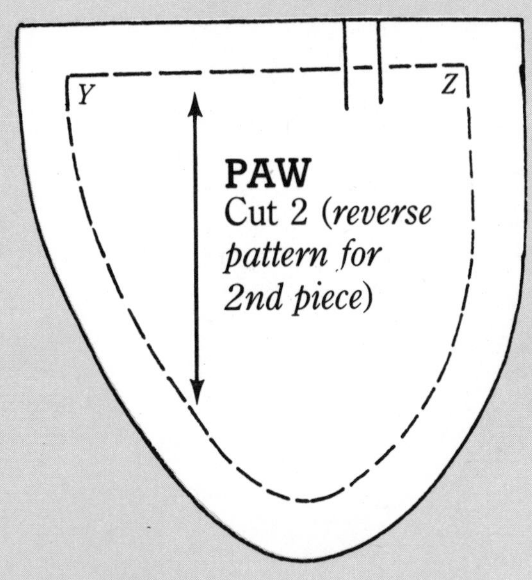
Y
Z
PAW
Cut 2 (*reverse pattern for 2nd piece*)

BABY BEAR

Baby is sewn in a lighter fur fabric than Papa or Mama. Like all babies she has a newborn's beautiful blue eyes.

MATERIALS NEEDED

The materials needed are the same as those for Papa (see page 42) with only the following changes:

Fur fabric for bear: 11 x 36 inches

Fabric for pads and paws: 5 x 7 inches

1 bag of stuffing (16 oz.)

1 pair of glass eyes, 12 mm in diameter

BABY'S PATTERN

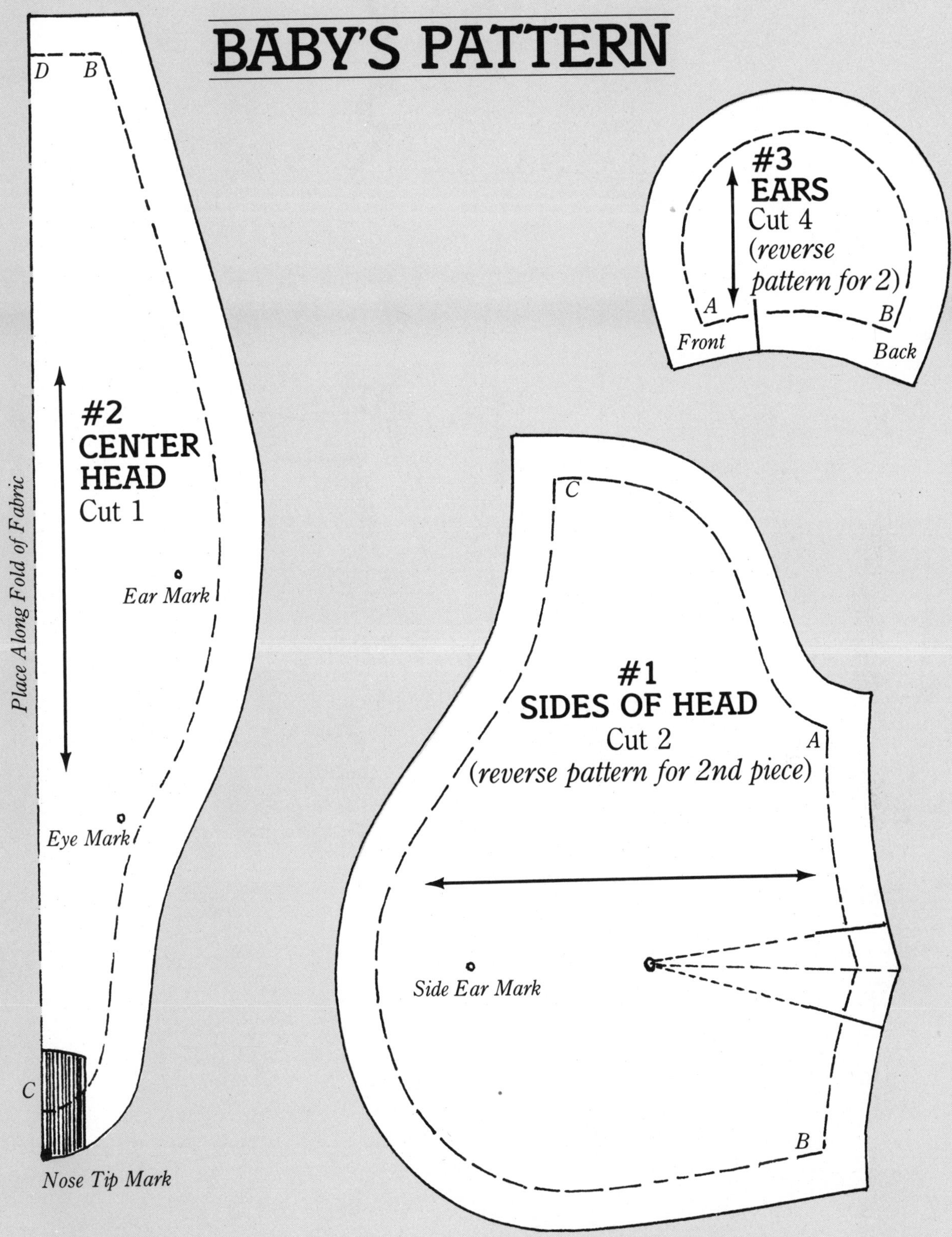

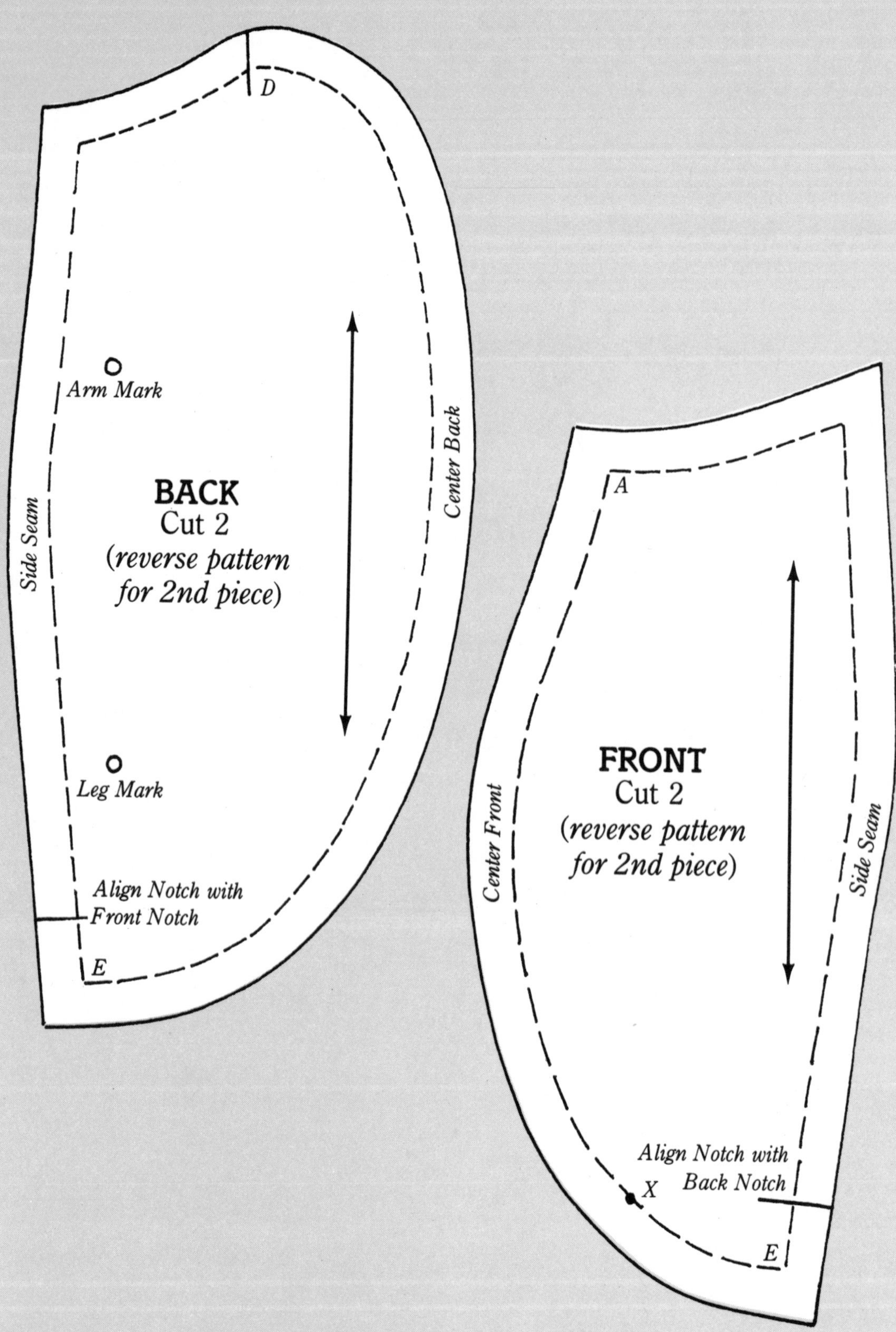
D
Arm Mark
Center Back
BACK
Cut 2
(reverse pattern
for 2nd piece)
Side Seam
Leg Mark
Align Notch with
Front Notch
E
A
FRONT
Cut 2
(reverse pattern
for 2nd piece)
Center Front
Side Seam
Align Notch with
Back Notch
X
E

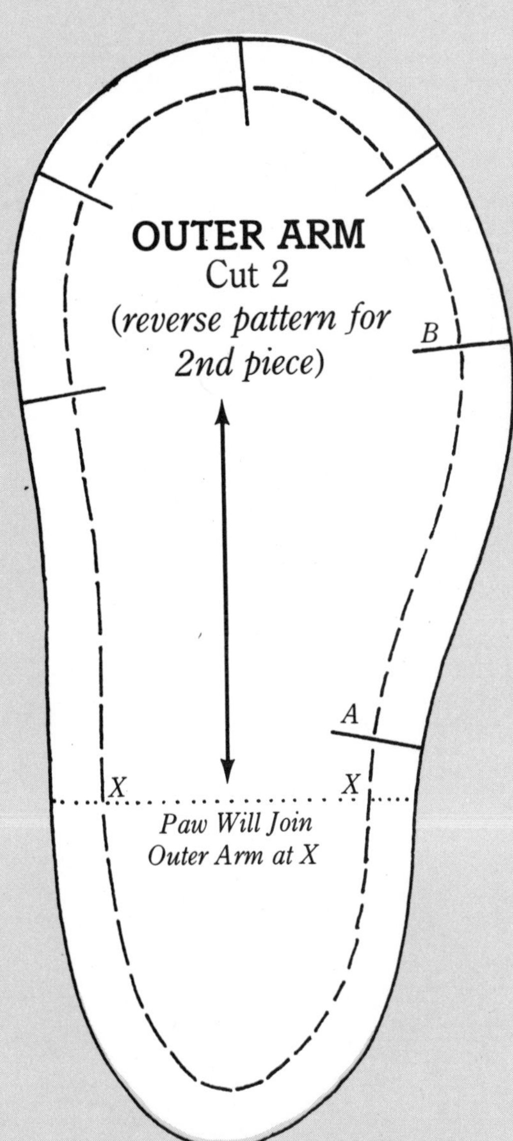
OUTER ARM
Cut 2
(reverse pattern for
2nd piece)
B
A
X
X
Paw Will Join
Outer Arm at X

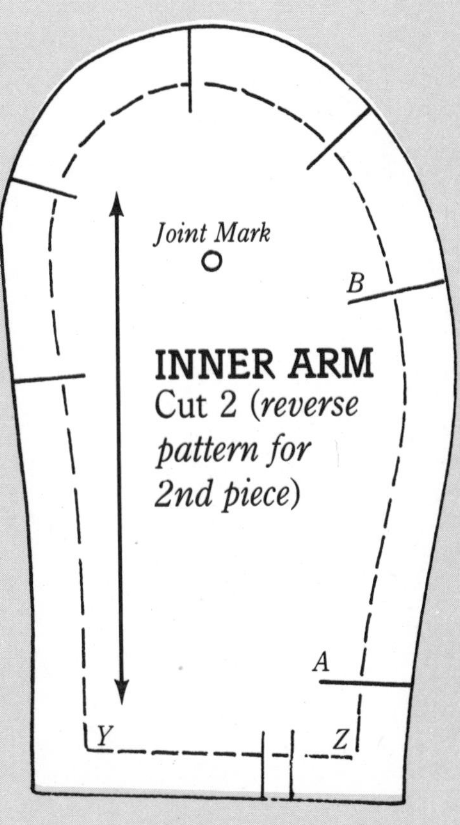
Joint Mark
B
INNER ARM
Cut 2 (reverse
pattern for
2nd piece)
A
Y
Z

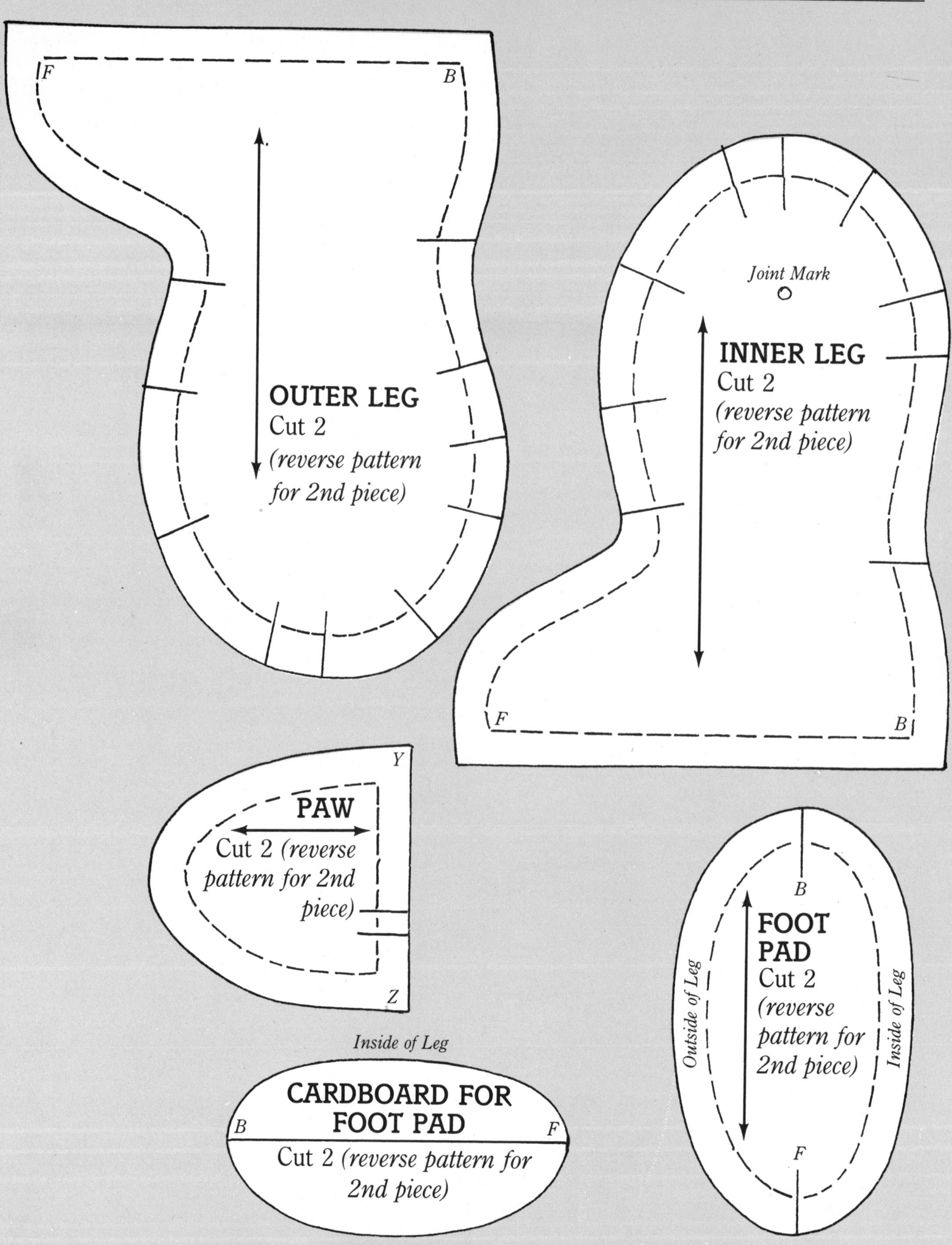
F
B
OUTER LEG
Cut 2
(reverse pattern
for 2nd piece)
Joint Mark
INNER LEG
Cut 2
(reverse pattern
for 2nd piece)
F
B
Y
PAW
Cut 2 (reverse
pattern for 2nd
piece)
Z
B
FOOT
PAD
Cut 2
(reverse
pattern for
2nd piece)
F
Outside of Leg
Inside of Leg
Inside of Leg
CARDBOARD FOR
FOOT PAD
B
F
Cut 2 (reverse pattern for
2nd piece)
Outside of Leg

TEDDY BEAR WARDROBE

Papa's Sweater

Papa's Collar and Tie

Mama's Apron

Mama's Bonnet

Baby's Presentation Gown

Baby's Everyday Dress

PAPA'S SWEATER

Papa's Tyrolean sweater jacket is designed to be made from a man's crew-neck or V-neck sweater. If you haven't got an old one lying around that is no longer being worn, you can probably find one for pennies in a thrift store or at a garage sale.

The pattern is on page 65.

MATERIALS NEEDED

- Long-sleeved pullover sweater, in a large size
- 6 domed "brass" buttons, ½ inch wide
- 5 inches of velvet ribbon, ¼ inch wide
- 10 to 12 small artificial flowers and leaves
- Sewing needles, various lengths
- Thread to match

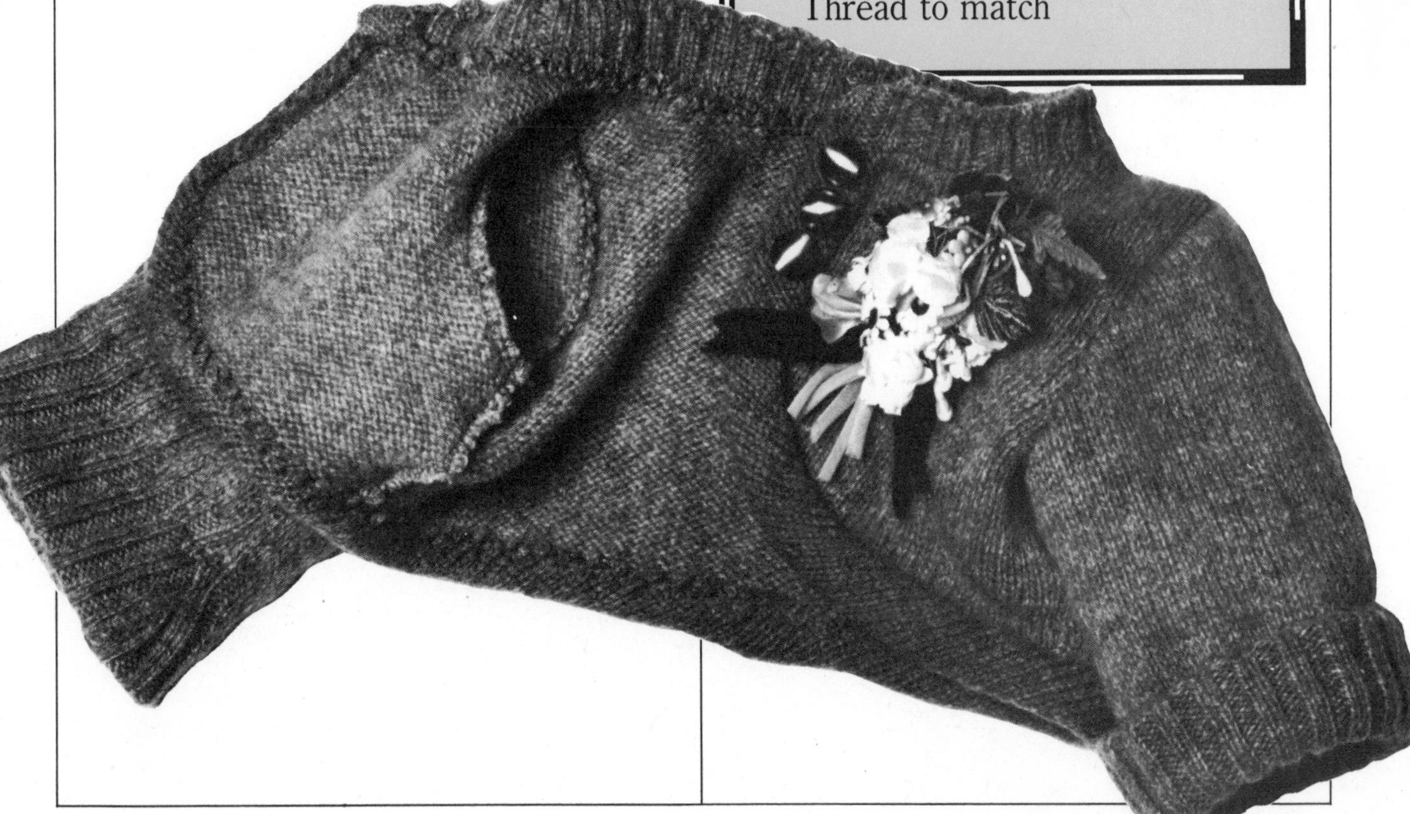

1

Following the directions on page 25, enlarge the pattern for the body of the sweater. Transfer the pattern to a folded piece of tracing paper, as shown in *Fig. 1.* Cut out the pattern and unfold the paper. Now you have a complete sweater body pattern *(Fig. 2).*

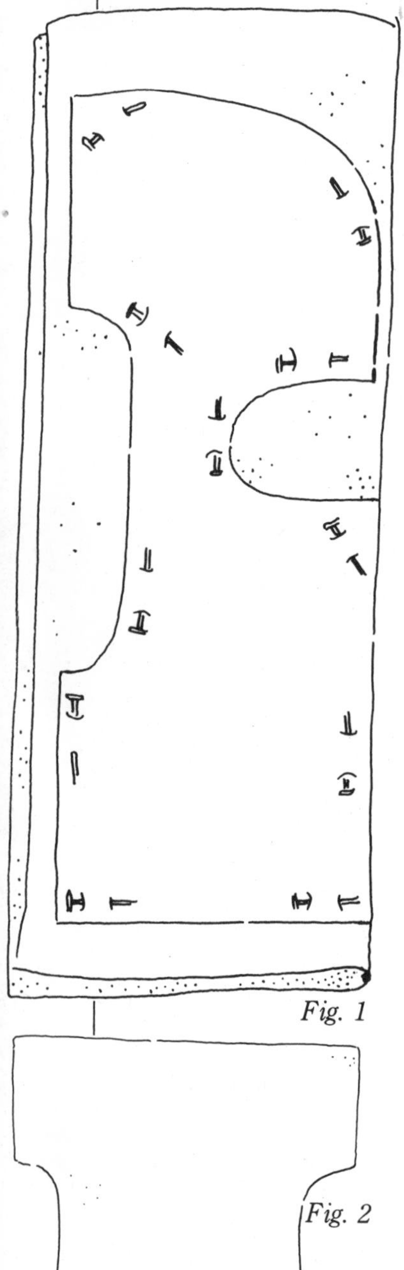

Fig. 1

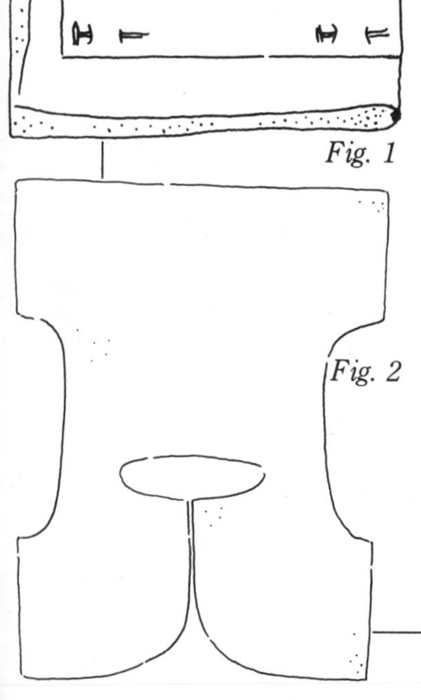

Fig. 2

2

Trace the sleeve pattern from the book onto tracing paper. Cut this out and use it as your pattern. Set the pattern pieces aside.

3

Cut off the sweater sleeves at the shoulder seams, and also cut off the ribbing at the bottom of the sweater. Be careful to keep the sweater from unraveling. Set the sleeves and ribbing aside.

4

Place the body section of the sweater, right side out, on a flat surface, and smooth it out. Place, then pin the body pattern piece onto your sweater. Cut the piece out, making certain to cut only through one layer of sweater.

5

From the remaining portion of the sweater body, measure and mark a bias strip 1½ x 28 inches (see page 64). Cut out the strip. If need be, cut a second bias strip and sew them together to make the 28-inch length (remember to leave a ¼-inch seam allowance for each piece so that the final length does not fall short of 28 inches). Set the strip aside.

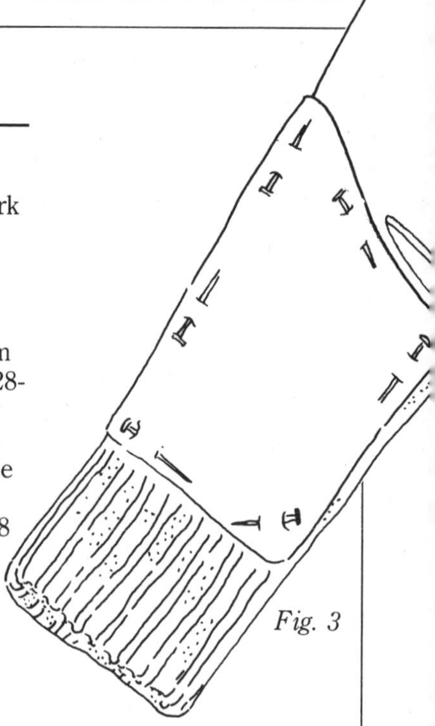

Fig. 3

6

Take the 2 sweater sleeves, right side out, and lay them out flat and smooth, one sleeve on top of the other. Make certain both sleeves are flush with each other and that both underarm seams are at the bottom edge. Place the sleeve pattern on top of the fabric so that the straight end of the pattern *(A-B)* runs along the edge of the ribbing where it joins the sleeve and *B-C* runs along the bottom edge (the seam edge). Pin the pattern to the fabric and cut out along the curved edge of the pattern *only*, cutting through both sleeves at once *(Fig. 3).*

7

Take the body piece and pin the sides together, wrong side out, from the bottom of the armhole to the bottom of the sweater *(Fig. 4).*

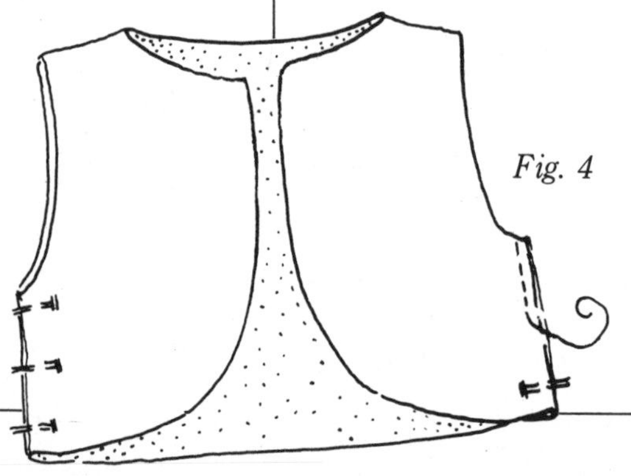

Fig. 4

8

Working in small stitches close to the fabric edges, back-stitch through both layers from the armhole to the sweater bottom along one side. As you sew do not stretch the fabric out of shape. Along the same side of the sweater, buttonhole-stitch from armhole to bottom. This will ensure that the sweater will not unravel. Repeat both sewing steps on the other armhole edge.

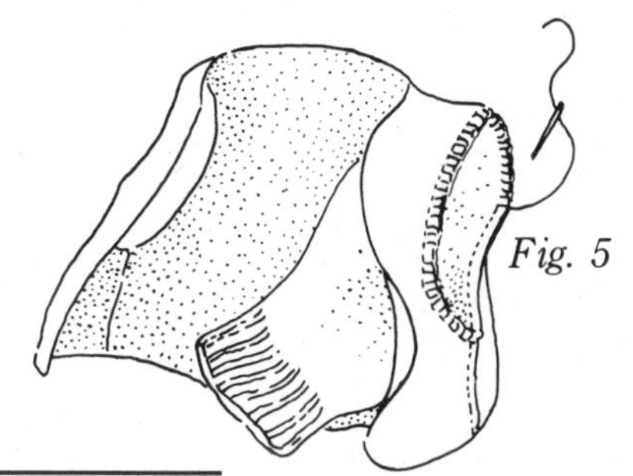
Fig. 5

9

With the sweater body still wrong side out, pin the sleeves in, following *Fig. 5*. You will note that it is unnecessary to turn the sleeves wrong side out. Just leave them as is. Be sure to line up the underarm seams of the sleeves with the side seams of the sweater. As you pin past the *X* mark, ease in the sleeve fabric. When both sleeves are pinned in, back-stitch and then buttonhole-stitch the fabric edges as you did with the side seams of the sweater body.

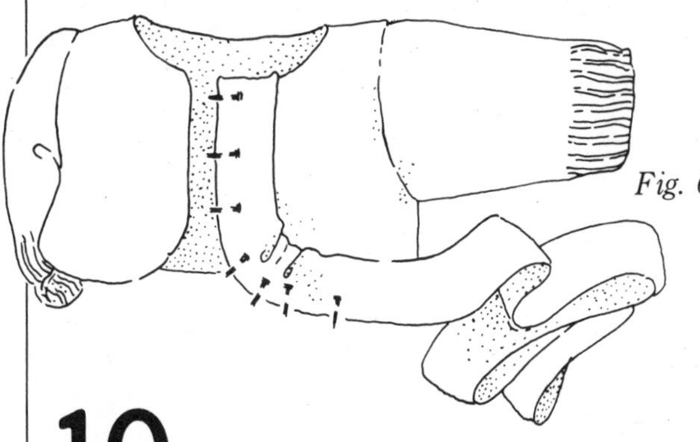

Fig. 6

10

Turn the sweater right side out. Starting at the top of one side of the front opening, pin the bias strip to the sweater. The right side of the strip should face the right side of the sweater *(Fig. 6)*. When you reach the curved bottom, ease the strip around the curve so it does not pull. Continue to pin all around the sweater's bottom edge, across the back, and finish on the other side at the neck, clipping off any excess bias material. You will not have pinned any of the strip around the neck opening. Using a ½-inch seam allowance, machine-stitch the strip to the sweater.

11

Turn the body of the sweater to the wrong side. Open out the bias strip and bring it around to the wrong side of the sweater *(Fig. 7)*. Start pinning at the top of one side of the front opening and continue pinning as you did in step 9. Bring the edge of the strip only as far as the edge of the machine-stitch line on the sweater. Using a small herringbone stitch, sew the strip to the sweater, catching the strip with the bottom part of the stitch and the sweater with the top part of the stitch *(Fig. 8)*.

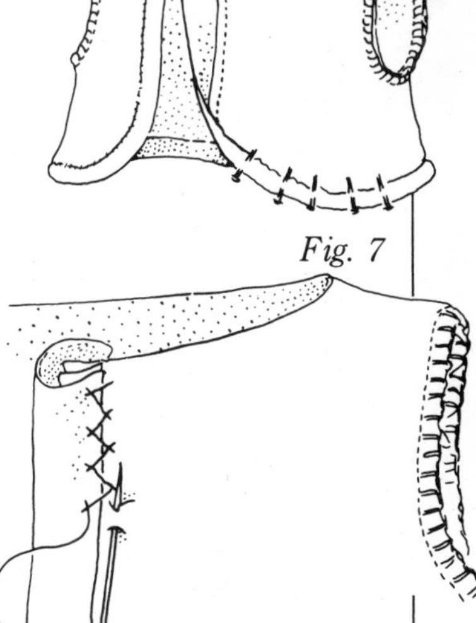
Fig. 7

Fig. 8

12

Now take the ribbing cut from your sweater bottom. Measure, then mark ¾ inch in from the finished edge. Cut a strip 12 inches long by ¾. With your sweater turned right side out lay the ribbing on the sweater. Line the raw edge of the ribbing along the raw edge of the sweater neckline. Leave a good extra inch of ribbing length at both ends of the neck. Pin the ribbing to the sweater.

13

Sewing close to the edge of the fabric, back-stitch the ribbing to the sweater, then finish off the seam by going over it with a row of buttonhole stitches.

14

Turn the sweater wrong side out. Pull the ribbing up and gently steam it with an iron. Allow the ribbing to dry, then fold down the front ends as in *(Fig. 9)*. Trim off any ribbing that goes below the seamline. Back-stitch along the bottom edge of the ribbing, then finish with very small herringbone stitches all around the neck ribbing.

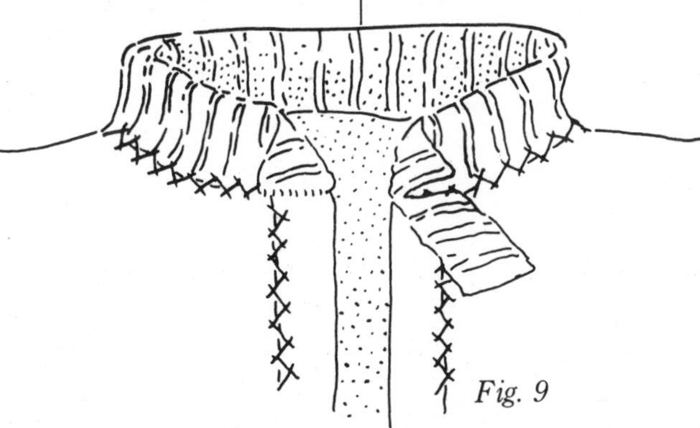
Fig. 9

15

Turn the sweater to the right side. Sew a button on one side just below the neck ribbing and in the middle of the bias edging. Space a second and then a third button just below, so they are very close together. Repeat the 3 buttons on the opposite side.

16

Form a nosegay with the artificial flowers and tie them securely with thread. Tie a loose knot in the center of the velvet ribbon and stitch it to the flower stems at the base of the flowers. Stitch the nosegay to the right sweater front in line with the bottom button. The sweater is finished and all that remains to complete Papa's outfit is his collar and tie.

CUTTING ON THE BIAS

Here is a very easy method to finding the bias of your fabric. Keep in mind that the fabric threads that run up and down (north and south) are called the warp. The threads that run from side to side are called the weft.

1

Cut across the bottom of your fabric, following a weft thread. This will ensure that the fabric is straight. Leave the selvage on both sides of your fabric (the warp).

2

Lay your fabric out flat and smooth. Lift one of the bottom corners and carry it almost completely across the fabric. Lay it flat on the fabric so that the selvage edge runs parallel with the weft threads. The folded diagonal line now forms the bias of your fabric *(Fig. 1)*.

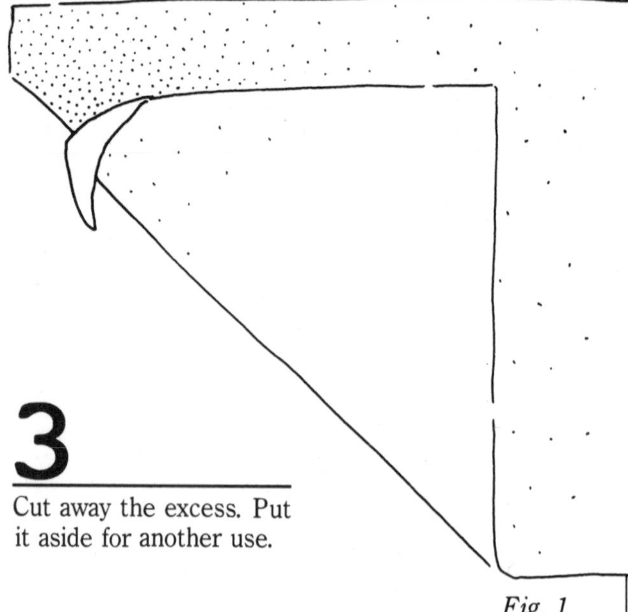

3

Cut away the excess. Put it aside for another use.

Fig. 1

4

After cutting away the small folded-over piece, use your ruler and mark with a sharp pencil or tailor's chalk along the diagonal bias line *(Fig. 2)*. Following pattern requirements, cut bias strips as needed in the width specified.

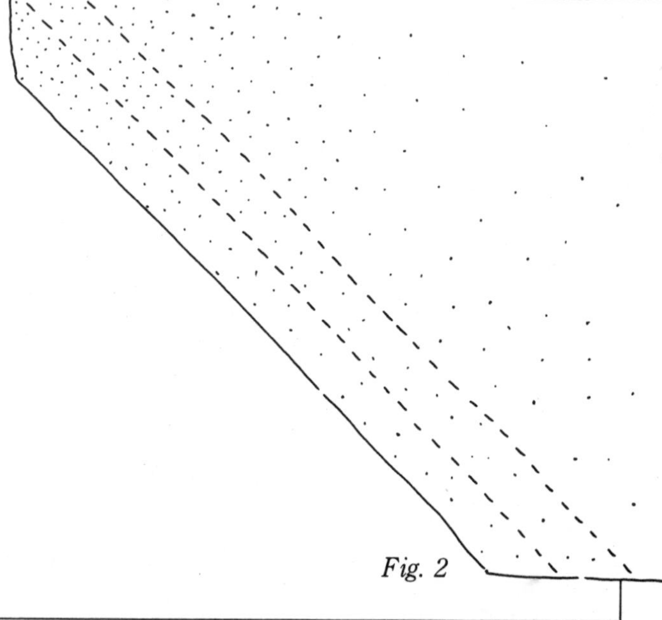

Fig. 2

Place Along Fold of Sleeve

A

SWEATER SLEEVE
Cut 2

Place Along Ribbing

PAPA'S SWEATER PATTERN

X

B

Place Along Sleeve Seam

C

1 SQUARE = 1 INCH

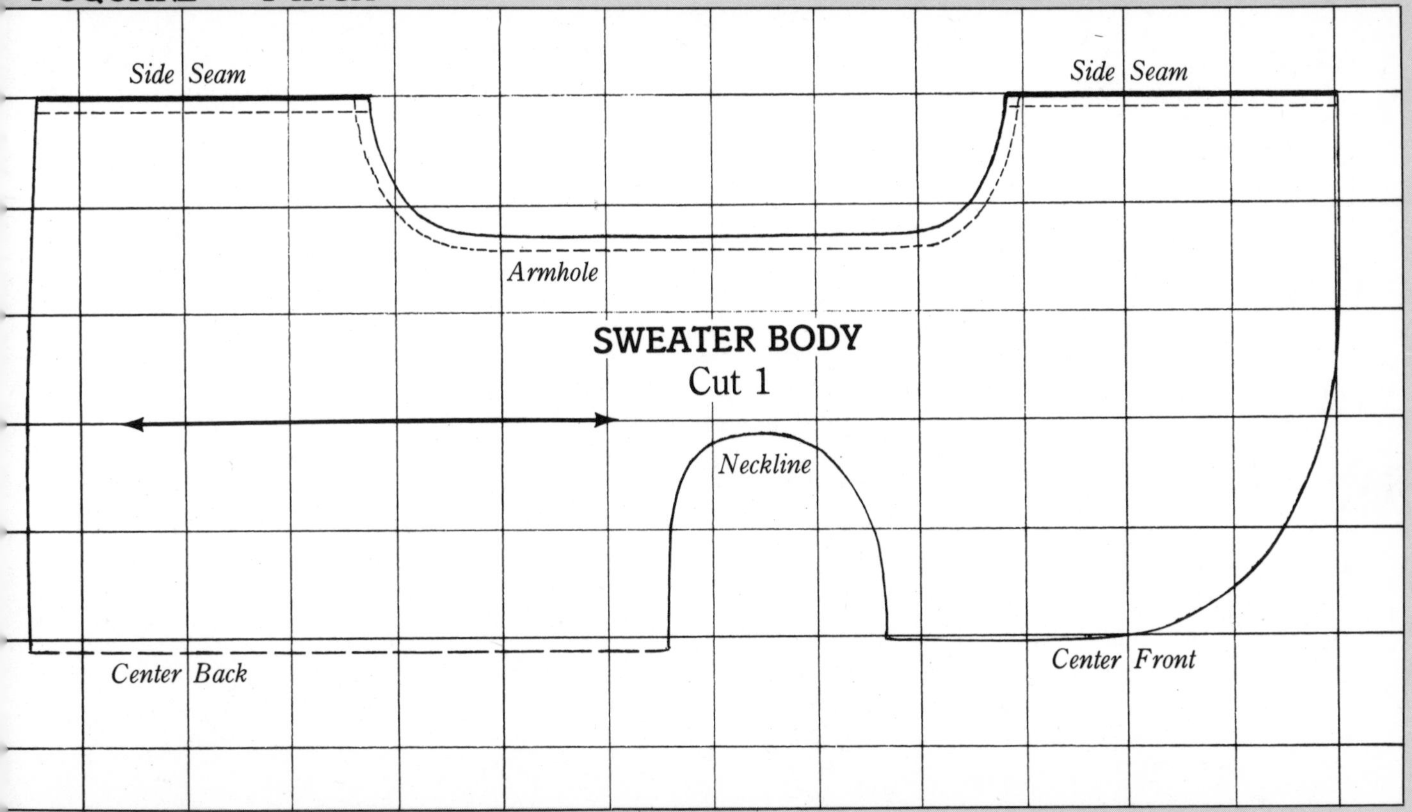

Side Seam

Side Seam

Armhole

SWEATER BODY
Cut 1

Neckline

Center Back

Center Front

PAPA'S COLLAR AND TIE

COLLAR

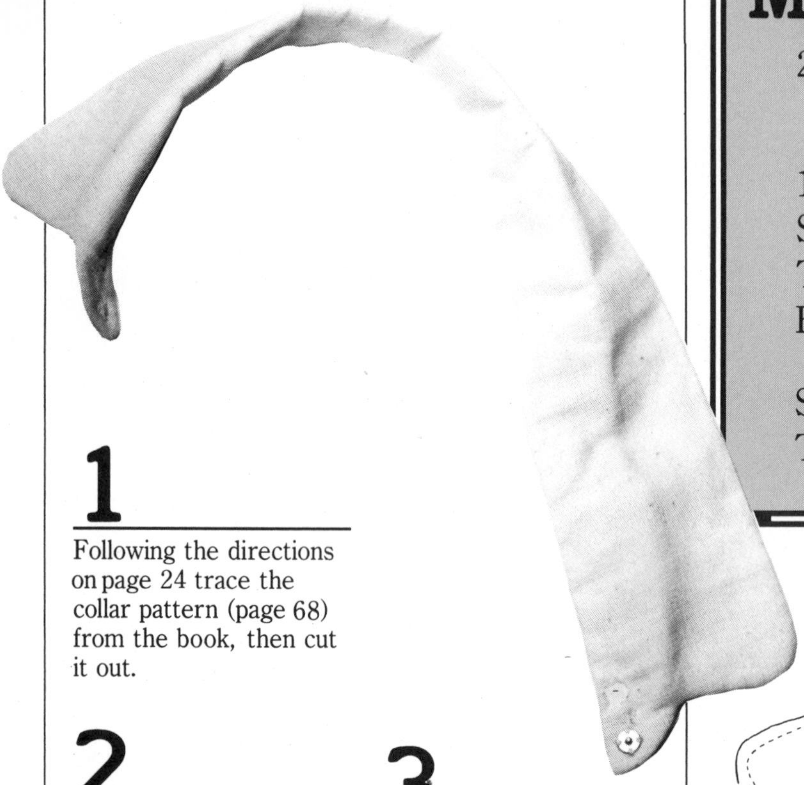

MATERIALS NEEDED

2 pieces of broadcloth or bleached muslin, each 4 x 15 inches
1 small snap
Sewing needle
Thread to match
Floral printed fabric, 4 x 26 inches
Sewing needle
Thread to match

1

Following the directions on page 24 trace the collar pattern (page 68) from the book, then cut it out.

2

Fold 1 piece of fabric in half, right sides facing in, and pin together. Place the collar pattern on the fabric, with the short straight edge on the fold, and trace the outline. Cut out the fabric. Repeat this with the second piece of fabric.

3

Open out the 2 collar pieces and pin them together, right sides facing in. Machine-stitch (or back-stitch) the long way around from *A* to *A*, leaving a ¼-inch seam allowance and locking seams at both ends. Then notch the curved end of the collar where marked. Trim the collar points close to the seam edge *(Fig. 1)*.

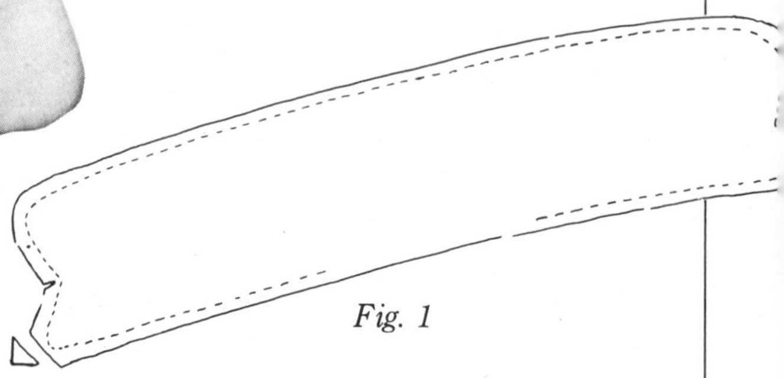

Fig. 1

4

Turn the collar to the right side and iron the seam flat. Slip-stitch closed the opening at the bottom of the collar between *A* and *A*.

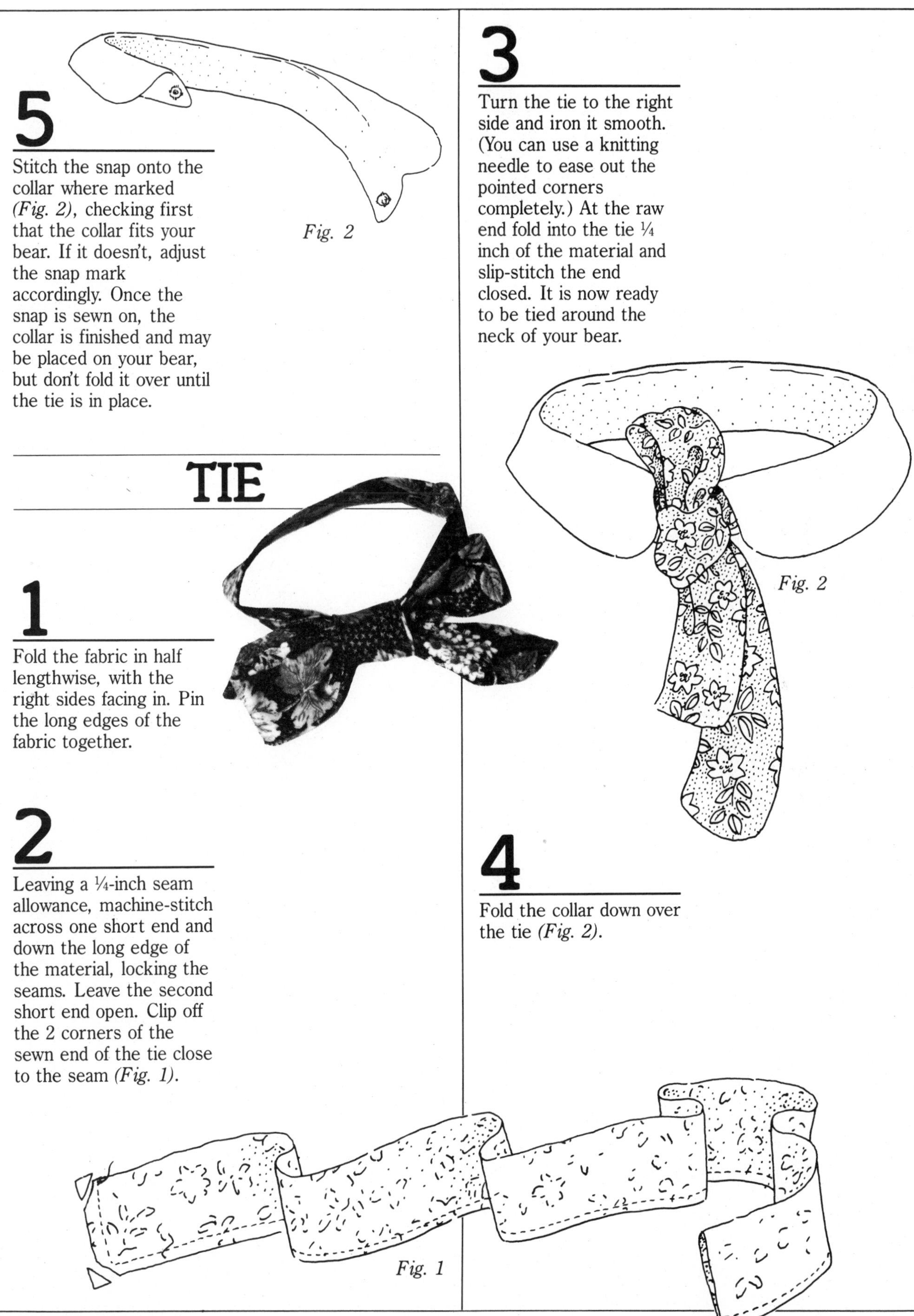

5

Stitch the snap onto the collar where marked *(Fig. 2)*, checking first that the collar fits your bear. If it doesn't, adjust the snap mark accordingly. Once the snap is sewn on, the collar is finished and may be placed on your bear, but don't fold it over until the tie is in place.

Fig. 2

TIE

1

Fold the fabric in half lengthwise, with the right sides facing in. Pin the long edges of the fabric together.

2

Leaving a ¼-inch seam allowance, machine-stitch across one short end and down the long edge of the material, locking the seams. Leave the second short end open. Clip off the 2 corners of the sewn end of the tie close to the seam *(Fig. 1)*.

Fig. 1

3

Turn the tie to the right side and iron it smooth. (You can use a knitting needle to ease out the pointed corners completely.) At the raw end fold into the tie ¼ inch of the material and slip-stitch the end closed. It is now ready to be tied around the neck of your bear.

Fig. 2

4

Fold the collar down over the tie *(Fig. 2)*.

Place Along Fold of Fabric
COLLAR
Cut 2
A
Snap Mark

MAMA'S APRON

Mama's apron was designed to be tied right under her arms, giving her a nice, high Empire waistline.

The pattern is on page 72.

MATERIALS NEEDED

Off-white cotton fabric, 12 x 36 inches
Light blue cotton fabric, 13 x 18 inches
24 inches of off-white lace trim, ½ inch wide
24 inches of pale olive green picot-edged ribbon, ⅜ inch wide
24 inches narrow pale olive green rickrack
Sewing needle
Threads to match

1

Following the directions on page 24 trace the border pattern pieces directly from the book, then cut them out.

2

Lay the off-white material on your work surface. Smooth it out, then measure and mark a piece 5 x 14 inches for the apron body. Measure and mark a second piece of off-white fabric 2 x 36 inches for the apron waistband and ties. Cut both pieces out.

3

Use the border pattern pieces to cut out 4 short and 2 long border pieces from the blue fabric.

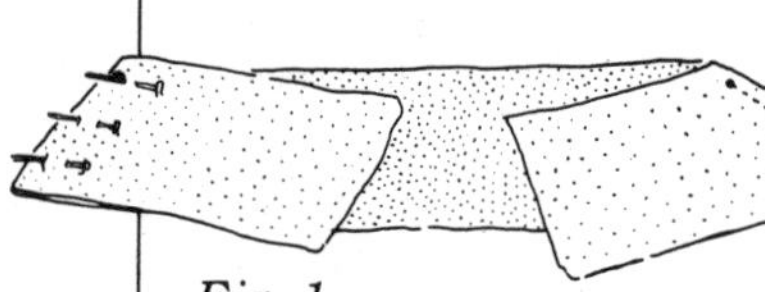

Fig. 1

Begin with the border. Take 1 long and 2 short strips. Lay the long section out flat, right side up. Next place the short pieces, wrong side up, on the long piece so that the curved ends of the short pieces are flush with the curved ends of the long piece *(Fig. 1)*. Pin the pieces together at these edges. Do the same thing with the other set of border pieces. Stitch the pinned edges as far as the *X*, leaving a ¼-inch seam allowance. Lock seams. Open out the seams and press flat.

5

Along the inside edge, fold ¼ inch of fabric over to the wrong side, baste, press, and set aside *(Fig. 2)*. Do this for both border sections.

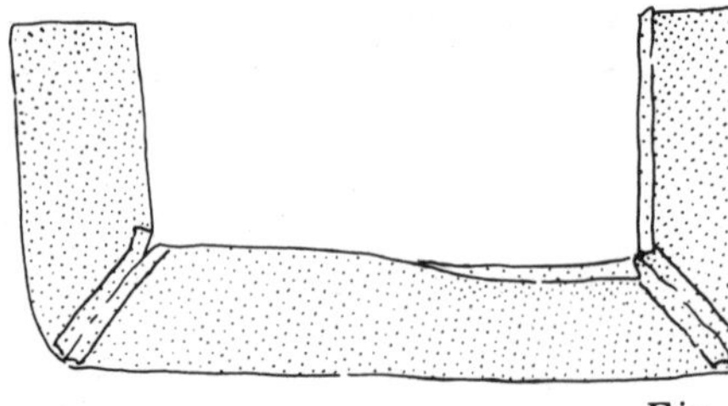

Fig. 2

6

Lay the white fabric out flat, right side up. Place one of the border sections, right side up, on top of the center piece, making sure it is about 1 inch in from the center piece edge on three sides. Pin the border to the center piece along the inside edge and top-stitch them together. The stitching should be at the very edge of the border *(Fig. 3)*. *Note:* There will be an excess of about 1 inch of the center piece extending beyond the border's seam allowance on the three sides. Leave it as is.

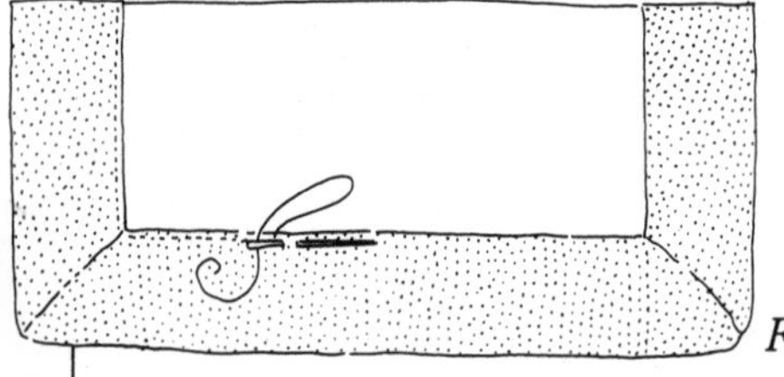

Fig. 3

7

Machine-stitch the lace to the apron, starting at *A*. The straight edge of the lace should be right at the edge of the border. As you approach the first corner of the border, ease the lace in so that it forms a slight gather and will turn the corner without pulling *(Fig. 4.)* Continue sewing the lace across the bottom, easing it around the second corner, and continue up the second side. Snip off any excess lace.

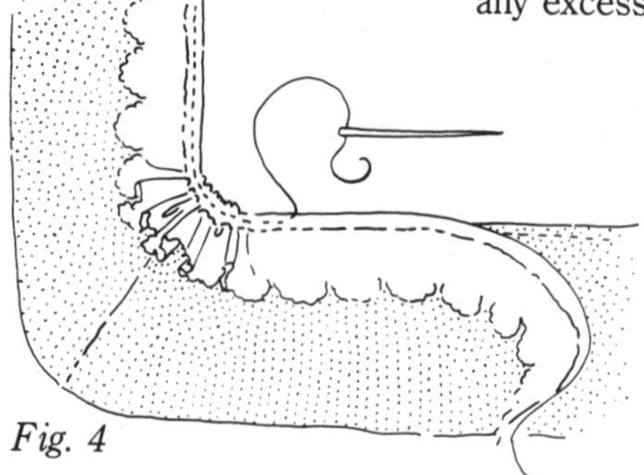

Fig. 4

8

Repeat step 7, this time using the picot-edged ribbon. Place the ribbon so that it overlaps the lace and extends into the center piece *(Fig. 5)*. Hand-sew or machine-stitch down the ribbon center. The ribbon seam should be almost on top of the lace seam.

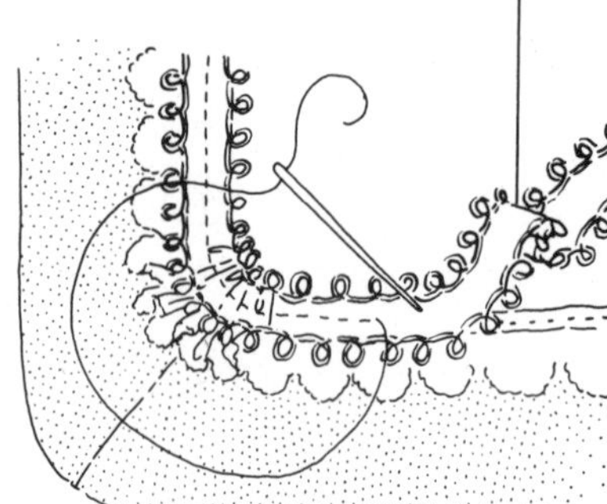

Fig. 5

9

The last piece of trimming to be added is the rickrack. Place the rickrack directly over the ribbon seam and hand-sew it to the ribbon *(Fig. 6)*.

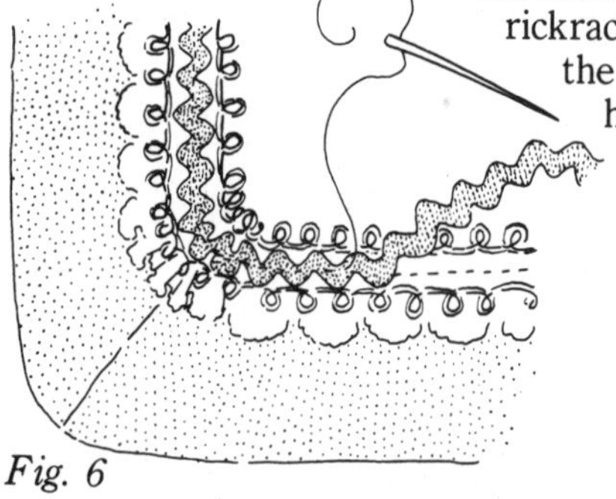

Fig. 6

10

Lay the apron flat, right side up. Take the second border section and place it on top, wrong side up, so that the corner edges are flush with the piece beneath. Pin all around the border edges, then sew them together, leaving a ¼-inch seam allowance *(Fig. 7)*. Trim the seams slightly, then turn the piece right side out. Press it flat, making sure the corners are rounded.

11

Along the back side of the apron, pin the inside edge of the border to the apron, and carefully slip-stitch the border to the center piece using small stitches, placing the stitches along the seam of the front border.

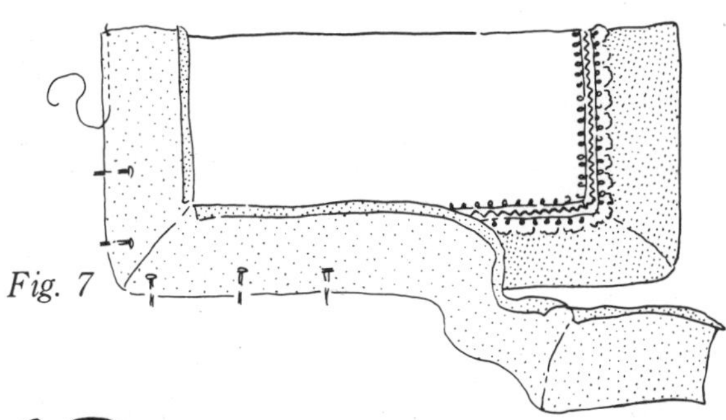

Fig. 7

12

Mark the center point along the top (unfinished) edge of the apron. Run a gathering stitch along this edge, about ¼ inch in from the edge. Pull the gathering thread until the apron top measures about 7 inches.

13

Take your waistband piece and mark the center point on it. With the right side of the waistband facing the right side of the apron, match this center point to the center point on the apron top (marked in step 12). Pin at this point. Then pin the rest of the waistband piece to the apron, allowing 3½ inches on each side of the center mark for the gathered apron top. Adjust apron gathers to fit as necessary. Stitch these pieces together, leaving a ¼-inch seam allowance.

14

Next, pull up the waistband, then fold over the 2 loose ends, right sides in. Pin along the raw edges up to the apron. Stitch along these edges *(Fig. 8)*, leaving a ¼-inch seam allowance. Lock-stitch. Do this on both ends of the waistband ties. Clip the corners at the ends, as shown.

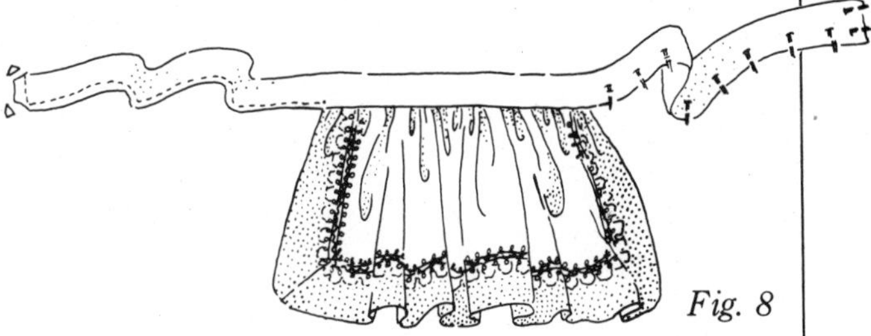

Fig. 8

15

Push the stitched ends of the waistband ties through to the right side, using a knitting needle to poke out the corners, and press flat *(Fig. 9)*. Place the apron on your work surface, back side up, and fold over the unsewn section of waistband, tucking under ¼ inch of the waistband material. Pin this section to the apron, and slip-stitch closed *(Fig. 10)*, using small stitches. Press this seam and touch up the entire apron, which is now ready for Mama.

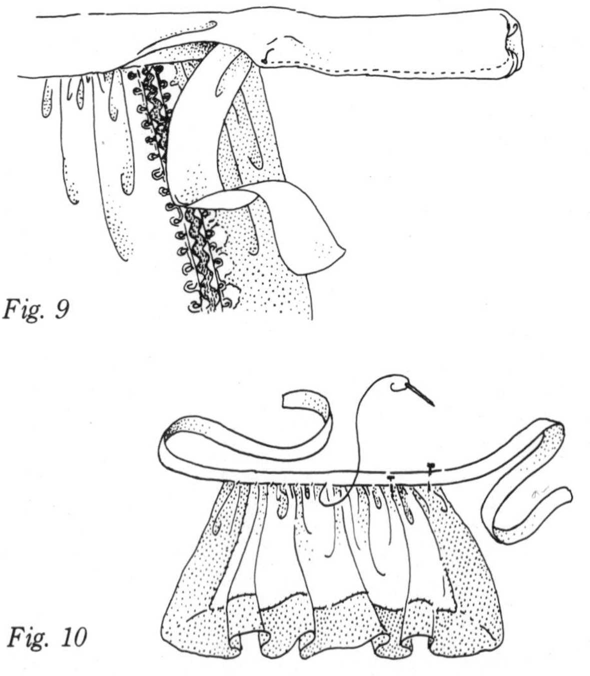

Fig. 9

Fig. 10

MAMA'S APRON PATTERN

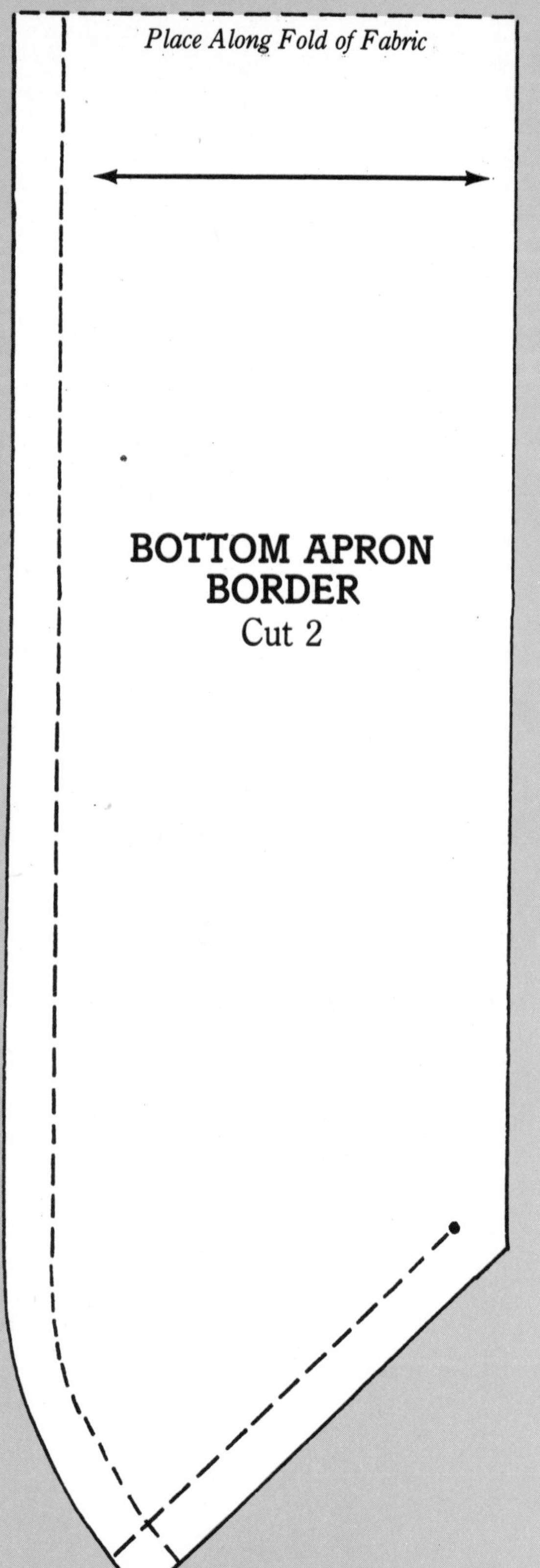

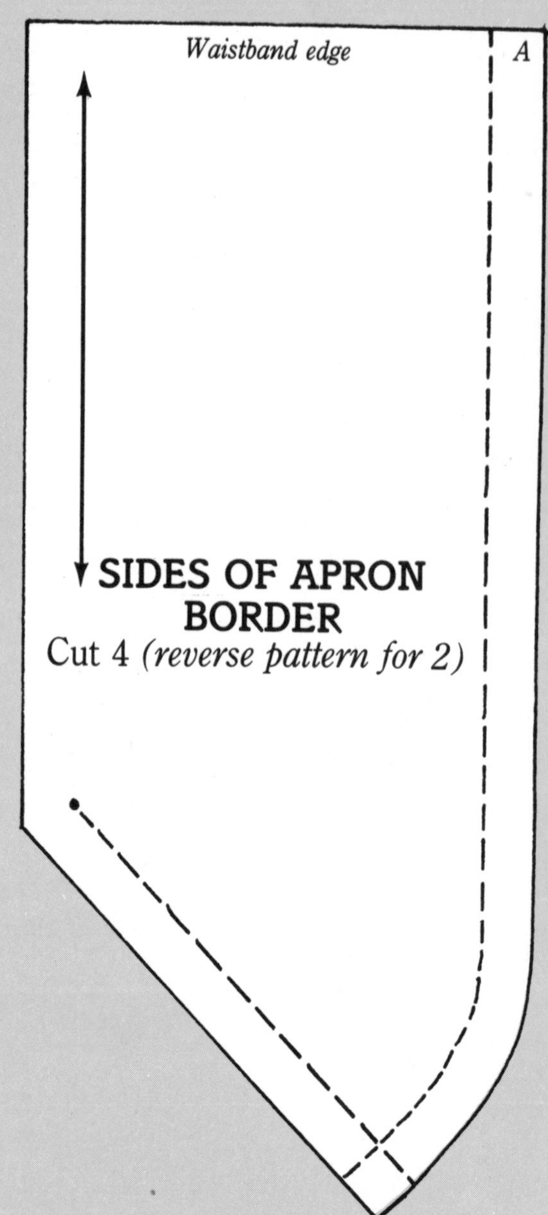

MAMA'S BONNET

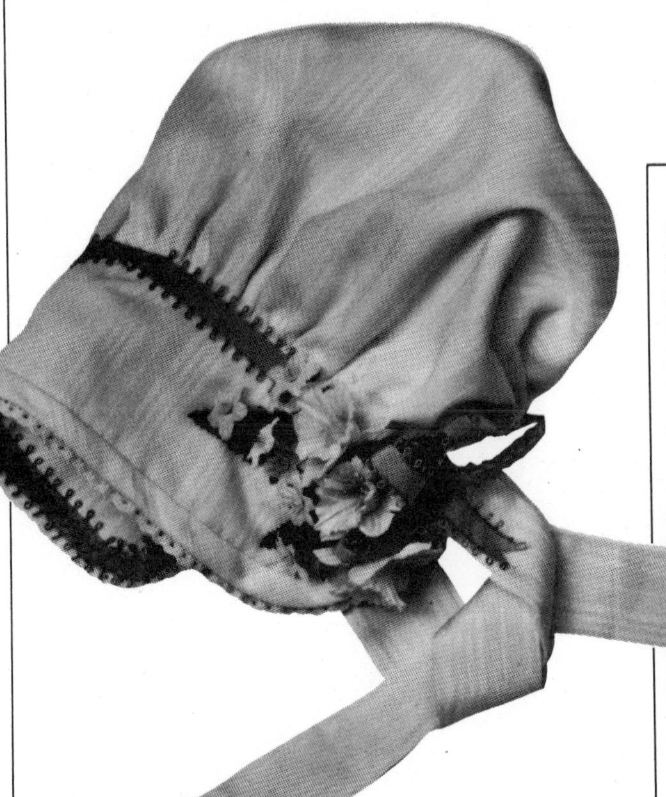

MATERIALS NEEDED

- Off-white cotton fabric, 36 x 36 inches
- Medium-weight white Pellon, 12 x 12 inches
- 18 inches of off-white lace trim, ½ inch wide
- 1½ yards of pale olive green picot-edged ribbon, ⅜ inch wide (optional)
- 18 inches of narrow pale olive green rickrack (optional)
- Assortment of small artificial flowers in white, yellow and lavender, with leaves (optional)
- Small hook and bar
- Sewing needles, various lengths
- Threads to match

1

Following the directions on page 25, enlarge the pattern grid for the bonnet (page 76). Transfer the pattern to tracing paper, then cut out the pattern.

2

Trace the brim pattern (page 77) from the book onto tracing paper, then cut it out.

3

Fold the off-white fabric in half and lay it out smooth and flat. Use the body pattern to cut out 2 body pieces from the fabric.

4

Use the brim pattern piece to cut out 2 brim pieces from the off-white fabric, then use the brim pattern to cut out 2 brim pieces from Pellon. Set aside for now.

5

From the off-white fabric measure and mark 2 pieces 3 x 13 inches. Cut them out. They will be the bonnet ties. Also measure and mark a bias strip 2 x 19 inches (see page 64). Cut it out. Set these pieces aside.

6

Place the 2 body pieces together, right sides facing in. Pin them along the vent. Using very small stitches, sew all around the vent *(Fig. 1)*. Trim the fabric, leaving approximately 1/16 inch seam allowance. Turn the pieces to the right side and iron the vent smooth.

7

Pin closed the remaining open edges of the bonnet, making sure both layers are smooth. Using a gathering stitch, sew across the straight side approximately 1/4 inch from the edge. Clip the thread, leaving an extra 3 inches at the end. Using a small stitch, and leaving a 1/8-inch seam allowance, sew from *B* along one curved side to approximately 1/2 inch from the vent. Clip the thread. Repeat this along the other curved side.

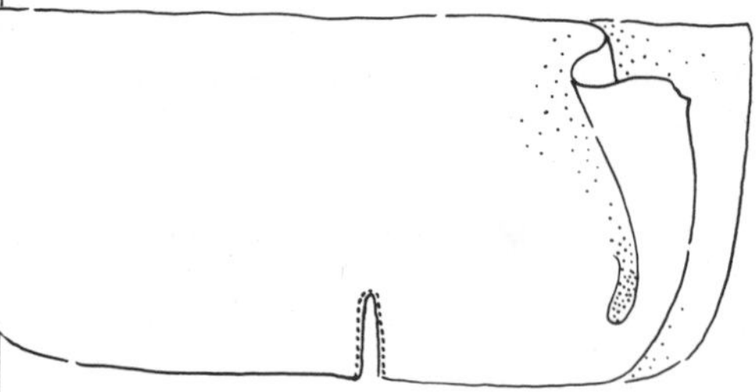

Fig. 1

8

Using a pencil, make a tiny mark at the center of the edge and at the center of the fabric brim pieces. Now pull the gathering thread along the straight edge of the bonnet until the material is gathered to the same length as the straight edge of the bonnet brim pieces *(Fig. 2)*.

9

Take 1 Pellon brim piece and 1 fabric brim piece and hand-baste them together with the right side of the fabric facing out. Do the same with the remaining Pellon and fabric pieces. From now on these pieces each will be worked as one piece.

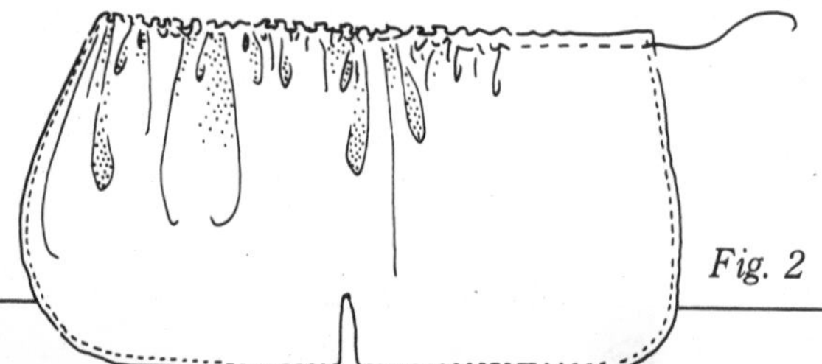

Fig. 2

10

Place one of the brim pieces on your work surface, fabric side up, with the straight edge at the top. Place the bonnet on top of the brim piece, gathered edge aligned with the straight edge of the brim. Place the second brim piece on the bonnet, fabric side down, and straight edge aligned with the others. Pin all 3 layers together *(Fig. 3)*. Leaving a 3/8-inch seam allowance, stitch the pieces together along the pinned edge; lock the seams.

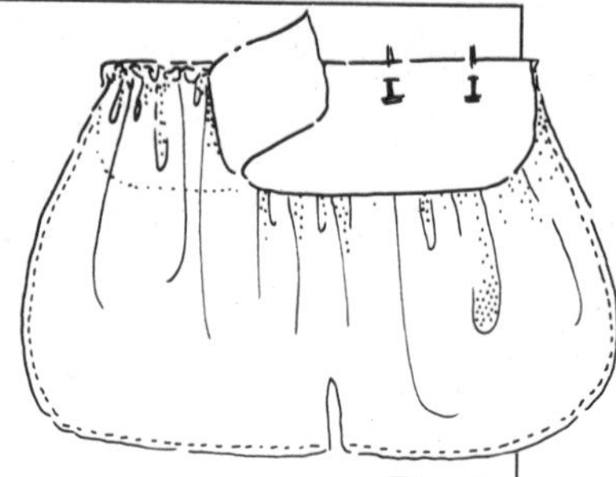

Fig. 3

11

Open out the brim pieces. Both right sides should be on the outside. Press the brim flat, but not the gathered bonnet edge. Pin the brim pieces together and top-stitch 1/4 inch in along the sewn straight edge.

12

Take the bias strip set aside in step 5, fold it in half lengthwise, and pin, then baste the raw edges together. On one end transfer the *A,B,C* marks from the notch chart, leaving a 1/2-inch excess at the end of the bias strip. Pin the bonnet at one side of the vent to the first mark *(A)* on the bias strip *(Fig. 4)*. The basted, raw edge of the bias should run along the raw edge of the bonnet. Letting the bias hang loose for the moment, pin pleats along that side of the bonnet, roughly at 1-inch intervals. Fold the pleats toward the vent. Adjust the size of the pleats, repinning as necessary until the pleated length *A-B* on the bonnet matches the bias length *A-B*. Pin the tucked fabric to the bias strip. Mark *C* on the strip lines up at the brim edge seam.

13

Continue pinning the bias strip all around the bonnet brim until you come to the second side of the bonnet. When you arrive at the brim seam, this will form mark *C*. Following the notch chart, measure and mark *B* and *A* as well, again leaving 1/2 inch excess at the end.

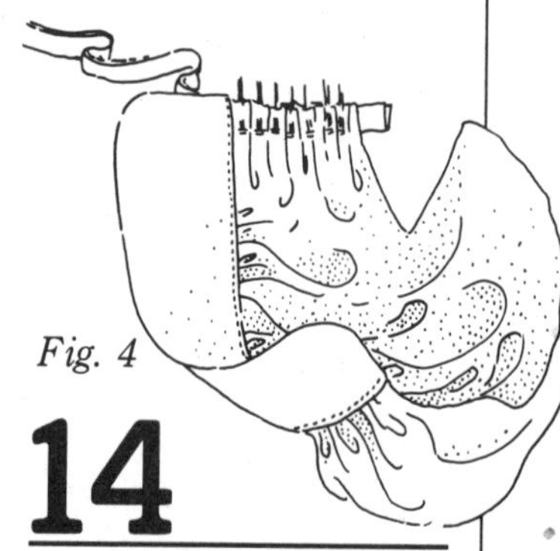

Fig. 4

14

Pleat this side of the bonnet between brim and vent, as you did in step 12. Pin the bias to the pleated edge.

15

Now stitch the bias to the bonnet, all the way around from vent to vent. Leave a ⅜-inch seam allowance *(Fig. 5)*.

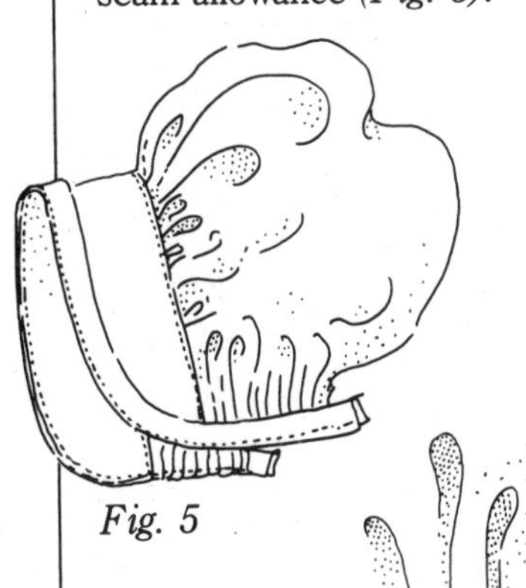

Fig. 5

16

Open out the bias strip. At the vent, fold the ½-inch excess over the bonnet's raw edge and pin. Do this at the other vent. Then fold up the bias. Pin, and continue pinning all the way around to the other side of the vent.

Fig. 6

17

Using small stitches, slip-stitch the bias strip to the bonnet, beginning at one side of the vent and ending at the other *(Fig. 6)*. Steam bias (only) lightly.

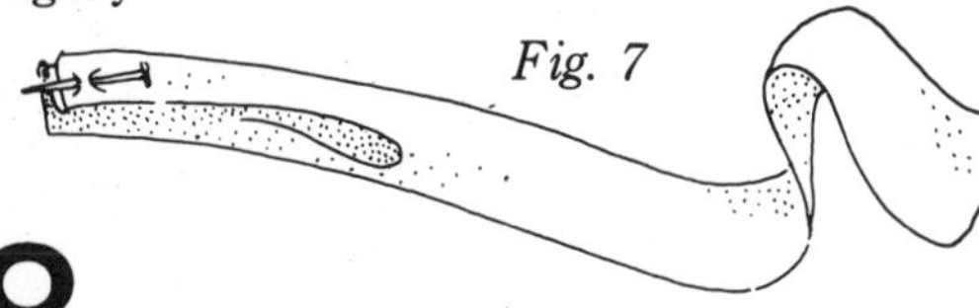

Fig. 7

18

First read "Trimming the Bonnet" and add lace trim if desired. Take the bonnet ties set aside in step 5. Fold each piece in half lengthwise, wrong side out, and pin long sides together. Sew up the long side, leaving ¼ inch seam allowance, and across one end. Turn the ties right side out and steam-iron flat. Fold in ¼ inch of the raw end and pin. Make a large tuck in that end of the tie *(Fig. 7)* and pin. Pin the tucked end of each tie to the inside of each side of the bonnet brim where it joins the bonnet. The end of the tie should just meet the bias strip on the bonnet *(Fig. 8)*. Slip-stitch the ties to the bonnet.

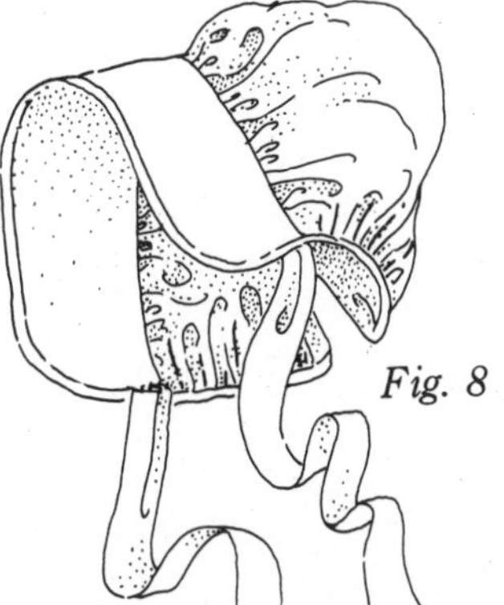

Fig. 8

19

Sew a hook and bar to the vent *(Fig. 9)* and hook vent closed.

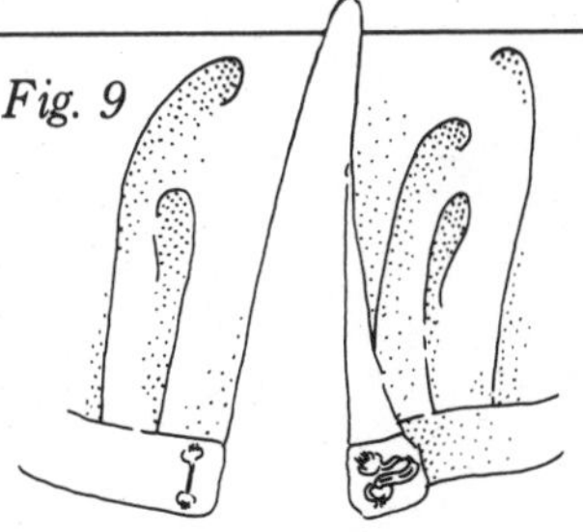

Fig. 9

TRIMMING THE BONNET

The bonnet is shown trimmed with picot-edged ribbon, rickrack and flowers, but the choice of whether or not to trim is yours.

1

To trim the bonnet as shown, before sewing on the bonnet ties, pin the length of lace trim just under the brim edge so the lace just peeks out. Be sure to ease the lace gently around the curved edges. Using a small running stitch, hand-sew the ribbon to the bonnet.

2

Pin a length of picot-edged ribbon just over the inner edge of the lace, again easing around the curved brim edges. Sew by hand with a small running stitch. Center and pin the matching rickrack on top of the ribbon and sew down with very small stitches *(Fig. 10)*.

3

If you wish to add the ribbon to the outside of the bonnet where the body joins the brim, pin a length of the ribbon at the center of that seam, at a 45-degree angle. Tack it down, then fold it over and bring the ribbon down along the seam to the brim edge *(Fig. 11)*. Clip any excess, leaving ½ inch to tuck under itself. Tack down the ends.

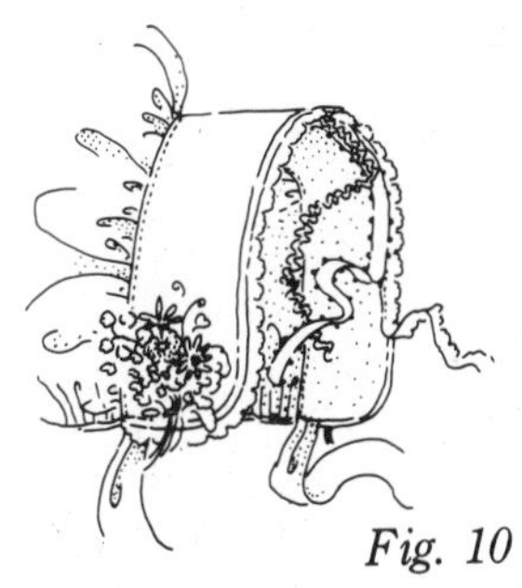

Fig. 10

Fig. 11

4

Add bows and flowers to each side of the bonnet, as desired. Add the bonnet ties as described in step 18.

1 SQUARE = 1 INCH

C
B
Back and side

BONNET BODY
Cut 2

Front
Vent
A
Center Mark
Place on Fold of Fabric

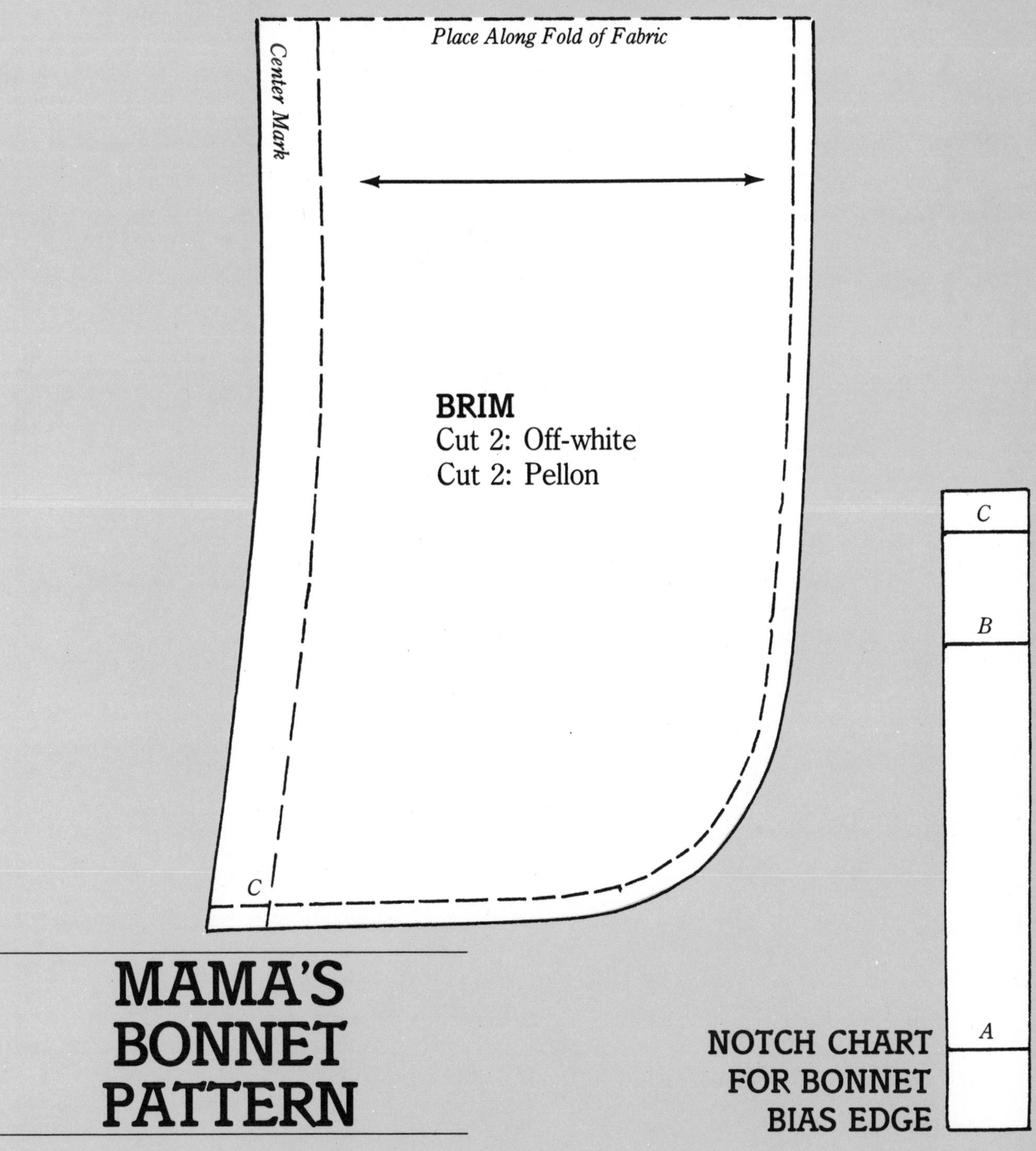

MAMA'S BONNET PATTERN

NOTCH CHART FOR BONNET BIAS EDGE

BABY'S PRESENTATION GOWN

Baby's presentation gown takes more time than the other bear outfits but it is not difficult to sew. The only pattern required is the sleeve, which you'll find on page 84.

MATERIALS NEEDED

- Thin pastel fabric, 24 x 36 inches
- Thin white fabric such as batiste or eyelet, 24 x 36 inches
- 26 inches of white insertion lace, 2 inches wide
- 25 inches of white lace trim, 3/8 or 1/2 inch wide
- 3 yards of narrow white rickrack
- 6 inches of ribbon, 1/8 inch wide
- 7 seam binding flowers (see Flower Trim, which follows)
- 5 self-shank pearl buttons, 1/4 inch wide
- Small hook and bar
- Sewing needles, various lengths
- Threads to match

1

Following the directions on page 24, trace the sleeve pattern from the book and cut it out.

2

Lay the pastel fabric on a flat surface and smooth it out. From the fabric cut:

1 dress piece 16 x 26 inches
2 sleeves using the tissue pattern
2 placket strips 1¼ x 4¾ inches
1 bias strip 2 x 12 inches

3

Lay the white fabric on a flat surface and smooth it out. From this fabric cut:

1 dress piece 9½ x 26 inches
1 dress piece 5 x 26 inches
2 sleeves using the tissue pattern

4

Put aside all except the 2 white dress pieces. Folding under ⅛ inch, baste 1 long edge of each of the 2 pieces. Fold under again and machine-stitch close to the top of the folded edge.

5

Pin the length of insertion lace to the right side of the 2 hemmed edges, so that each edge of the lace slightly overlaps the white fabric *(Fig. 1)*. Top-stitch the lace to the white fabric. When these 3 sections are sewn into one piece, lay the narrow rickrack over the top-stitching of the lace. Pin the rickrack in place, and top-stitch.

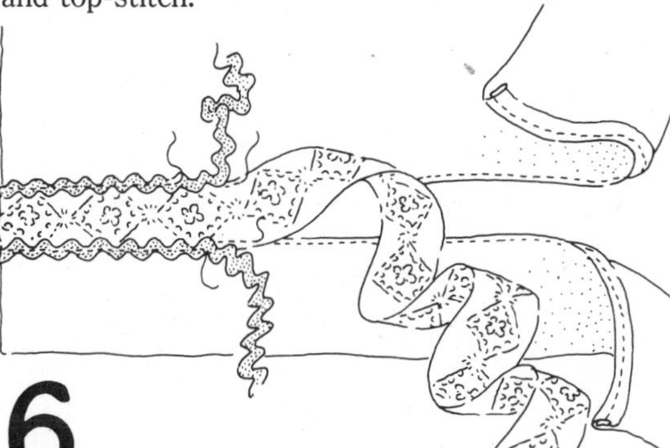

Fig. 1

6

Mark the center of the material at the top edge of the larger white piece. The mark locates the center front of the dress. The lace and narrow strip of white fabric now make up the hem end of the dress. Set aside.

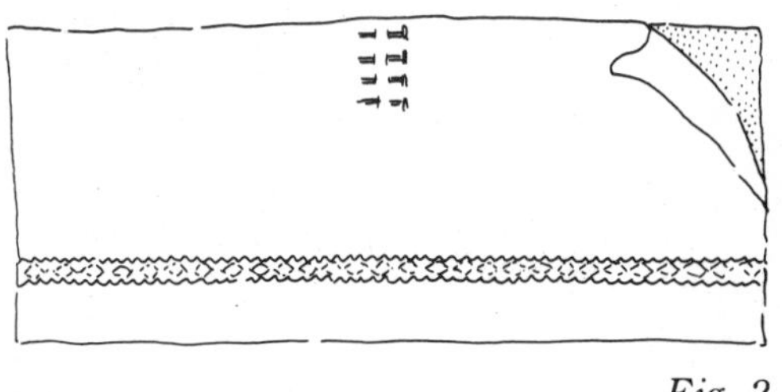

Fig. 2

7

Take the pastel fabric dress piece and mark the center point along 1 long edge. Lay the pastel fabric out right side up, smooth and flat. Over this place the completed white piece, right side up. Pin the fabrics together at the center-front mark *(Fig. 2)*.

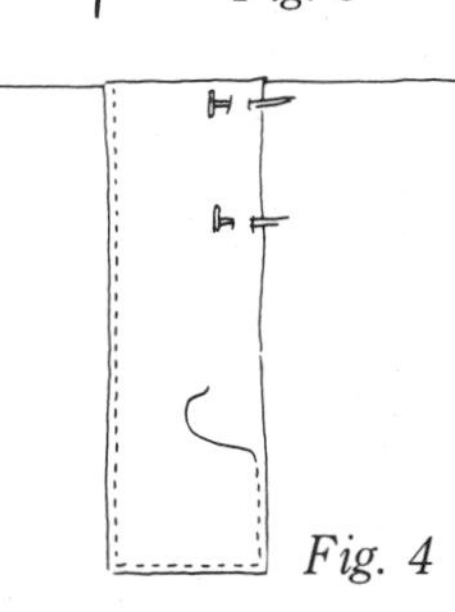

Fig. 3

Fig. 4

8

Take the 2 pastel placket strips, right side up, place them one on top of the other and, working them as one piece, fold under ¼ inch on each of the long edges. Pin, then baste these edges. Fold under ¼ inch at one short end, pin and baste. Place this strip, right side up, raw edge aligned with the raw edge of the dress, centered on the center mark of the dress *(Fig. 3)*. Pin the strip to both layers of dress fabric, making sure to first remove the pins that mark the dress center. Top-stitch the strip as close to the edge as possible *(Fig. 4)*. This piece is now the neckline placket of the dress.

9

Starting at the top of the neckline, place the ⅜-inch lace, right side up, so that the straight edge of the lace is on the placket top-stitching. Top-stitch the lace to the dress, easing and slightly gathering the lace when turning the 2 corners. Continue to stitch up the second side of the placket to the neckline *(Fig. 5)*. Clip off the remaining lace. Then pin the rickrack over the lace top-stitching, easing it around the corners. Top-stitch the rickrack.

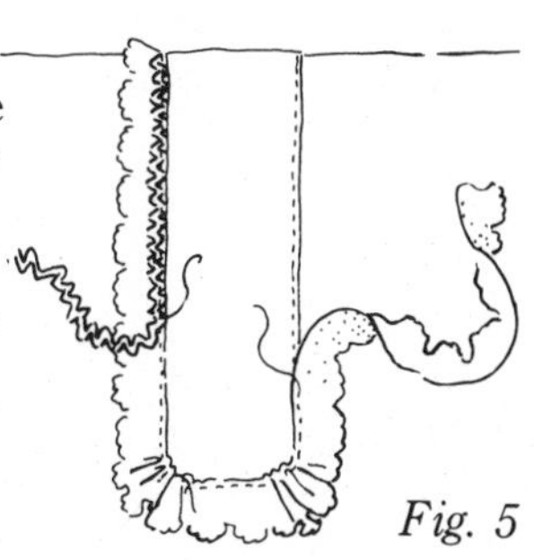

Fig. 5

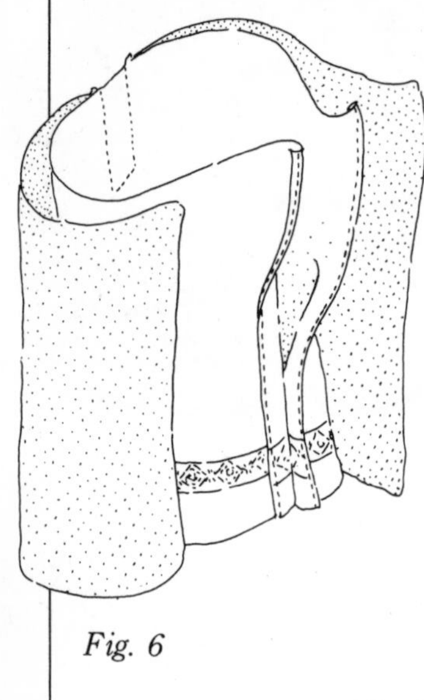

Fig. 6

Fig. 7

10

You are now ready to close up the back of the dress. Work the outer and inner fabrics separately, not as one piece. Measure and mark 6½ inches down from the top of one short edge on both fabrics. Leaving a seam allowance of 1 inch, machine-sew from that point to the hem of the white fabric *(Fig. 6)*. Repeat this on the pastel fabric. If you wish to finish the seams, either trim the cut edges with pinking shears, or fold the seams back ⅛ inch and top-stitch them from the neckline to the hem. Turn the dress so the white side is facing out. You now have 2 dress layers, one inside the other, joined together only where the placket is stitched, with the white layer on the outside *(Fig. 7)*.

11

To make the armholes, lay the dress out flat, placket side facing up. Line up the center back and the center of the placket. Smooth out the dress and folded sides, making sure the 2 layers of the dress are flush. Measure in at the top edge 1½ inches from one side of the dress and make a small mark. Next, measure 2¼ inches down from the top edge along the same side and mark. Place a ruler so that it is lined up with both marks *(Fig. 8)*. Make a light pencil line between the marks. Repeat this on the other side. After marking both sides, cut the fabric away along that line. Baste the 2 layers of each armhole together around the cut-out and lay the dress aside.

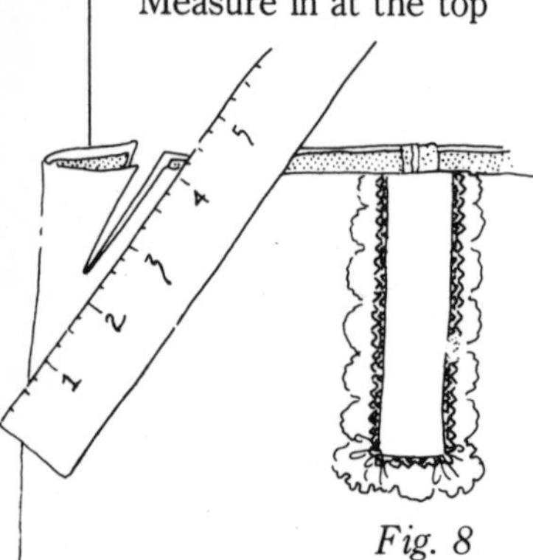

Fig. 8

12

Put the 4 sleeve pieces on your work surface. Cut 2 pieces of the ⅜-inch trimming lace as long as the longest edge of a sleeve piece. Fold each sleeve piece in half, wrong side facing out, and machine-sew together along the short edges, allowing a ¼-inch seam allowance. You will have 4 separate sleeve tubes. Next, make individual bands of each of the 2 strips of lace. Use French seams, leaving a $\frac{1}{16}$-inch seam allowance for each of the 2 parts of the French seam *(Fig. 9)*. You will now have 2 bands of lace in addition to the 4 sleeves.

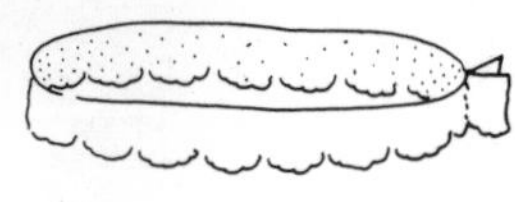

Fig. 9

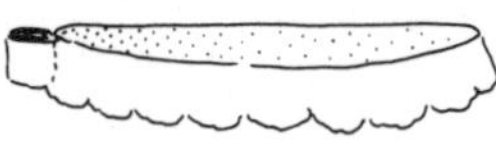

13

Turn both white sleeves right side out. Take 1 sleeve and 1 lace band, the French seam facing out. Slip the lace onto the sleeve so the straight edge of the lace is approximately ¼ inch up from the bottom edge. Pin, then baste the straight edge of the lace to the sleeve *(Fig. 10)*. Slip a pastel sleeve, wrong side out, over the white sleeve. Line up both sleeve side seams and pin the sleeves together around the bottom edge. Turn the sleeve to the white side and machine-stitch just above the basted lace seam *(Fig. 11)*. Pull the pastel sleeve from the inside of the white sleeve and over the white sleeve. Both sleeve seams should be on the inside and the lace should edge the bottom of the sleeve *(Fig. 12)*. Press the seam edge of the sleeve flat and turn it to the white side. Line up the top and armhole edges of the sleeve and baste them together *(Fig. 12)*. Repeat step 13 for the second sleeve.

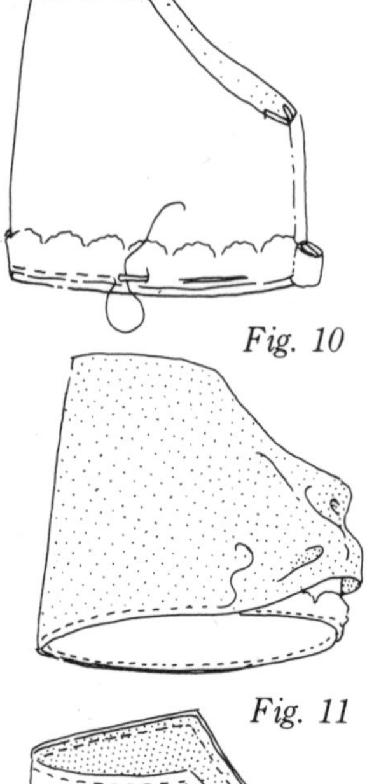

Fig. 10

Fig. 11

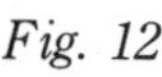

Fig. 12

BABY BEAR

Papa and Mama's greatest joy.

For special occasions, dress Baby in this delicate presentation gown made from an off-white batiste fabric with a pastel cotton underslip.

Baby goes nowhere without her rag doll bear, outfitted in a clownlike, double-edged white eyelet collar and ribbon bow.

Baby is called Plum-Plum because she is the "prize" of Papa and Mama's lives with her great big blue eyes, rusty brown nose and light, beige-colored fur. She is only a baby, so perhaps those blue eyes will grow darker and change, and her coat will become a deeper color with age and loving. She wears her blue and white everyday dress in the photograph, but you can also make up a beautiful presentation gown for special occasions. Plum-Plum never likes to go anywhere without her favorite Teddy Bear doll and comforting yo-yo blanket.

A short floral print for everyday wear. A ribbon may be added around the neck to complete the outfit.

Baby is just a cub, measuring only 11 inches in height.

Baby's brightly colored yo-yo blanket.

PORTRAIT OF YOUR TEDDY BEAR

Paste a photo of the first bear you complete in the frame below and keep it in this book as a permanent record. Write the bear's name in the space provided.

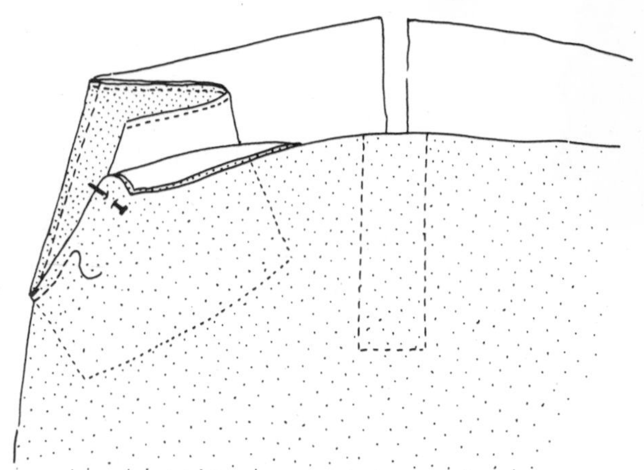

Fig. 13

14

Turn the dress so the pastel side is facing out. Take one of the sleeves, white side out, and slip it inside the dress. Line up the underarm sleeve seam with the point of the cut-away armhole *(Fig. 13)*. Pin in the sleeve, then place and pin in the other sleeve.

Machine-stitch along the pinned sections of both sleeves, leaving a ¼-inch seam allowance. Finish the seams by either pinking or buttonhole-stitching along the raw edges of fabric. Turn the body of the dress to the white side. It should look like *Fig 14*.

Fig. 14

15

Take the bias strip cut from the pastel fabric and fold it in half lengthwise, right side out. Pin, then baste it along the raw edges. Put aside.

16

With the white side facing out, run a gathering thread all around the neckline of your dress, approximately ¼ inch in from the edge. Start from the center-back opening and continue all around until you return to the opening. Do not clip the thread. Do make certain the center front of the dress is marked. Pull the gathering thread to evenly gather the dress neckline until it measures 10½ inches around.

17

Find the center of the bias strip and mark that point. Measure from the center 5¼ inches toward one end and mark that point. Repeat this along the other side. With the basted edge of the bias strip against the dress neckline, pin the center front of the dress to the center of the bias along the raw edges. Next pin one center back of the dress to the bias strip at the 5¼-inch mark. Repeat for the other side. If necessary, tighten or loosen the dress gathering to fit the length of the bias strip. Pin all around *(Fig. 15)*. Clip both ends of the bias, leaving approximately ½ inch extra at each end.

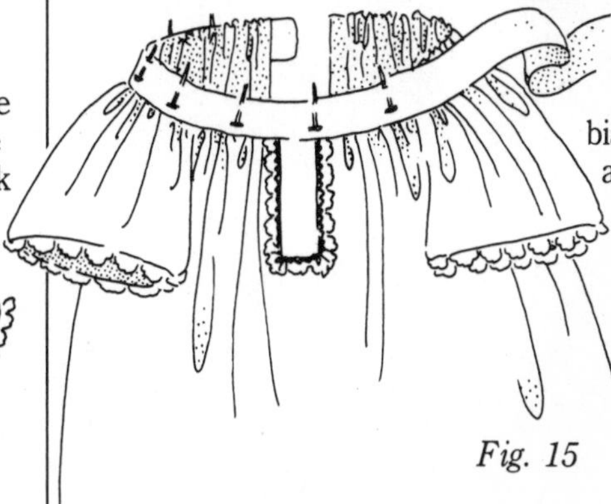

Fig. 15

18

Leaving a ¼-inch seam allowance, sew the bias and dress together at the neckline. Start at one back opening and continue around until you return to the opening. Turn the dress over so the pastel side is facing out. Pull the bias up, and fold the excess at both ends back onto the dress and pin *(Fig. 16a)*. Now fold down the bias to cover the raw edge all around the neckline and pin *(Fig. 16 b)*.

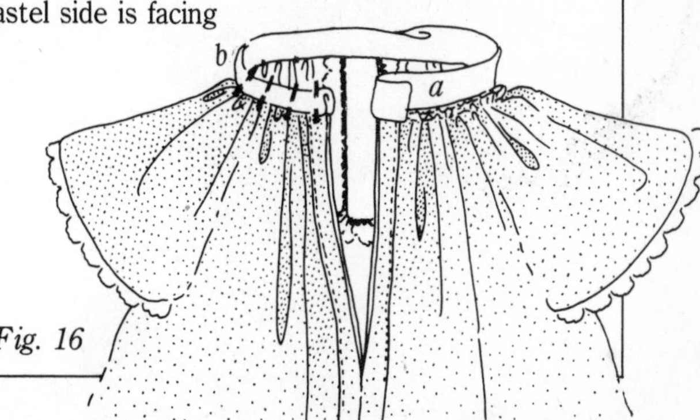

Fig. 16

19

Starting at the back center opening, slip-stitch the bias to the dress, using tiny stitches. Check to see that none of the stitches show on the front side of the dress.

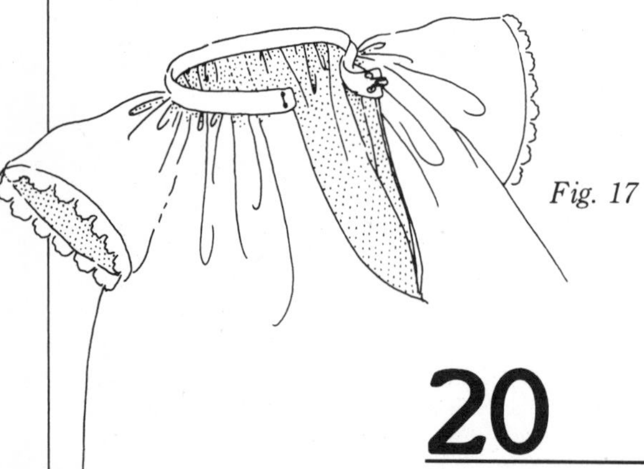

Fig. 17

20

Turn the dress so the white side is facing out and sew a small hook and bar at the back neckline, on the bias strip *(Fig. 17)*. Sew the pearl buttons down the center of the placket, placing the first button right under the bias neck edge. The remaining buttons should be placed approximately ¼ inch apart, depending on the size of your buttons. Lastly, tie a small bow with the ribbon and stitch it to the bias edge, just above the first button *(Fig. 18)*.

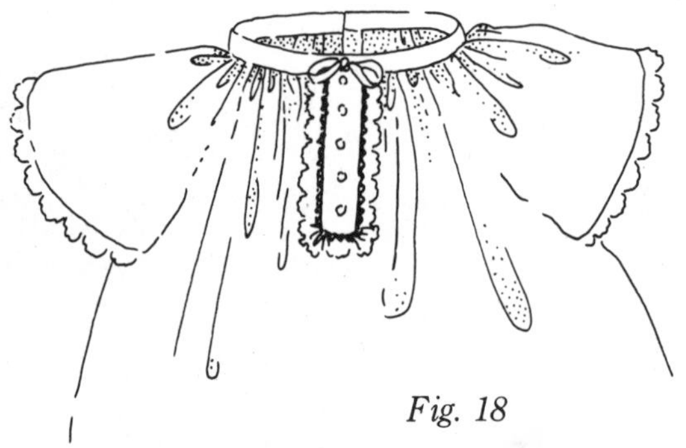

Fig. 18

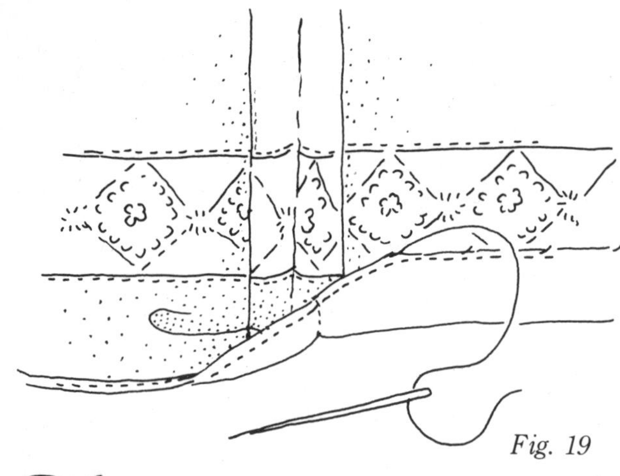

Fig. 19

21

To hem the dress, work each layer as a separate garment. Begin with the white one, which should be facing out. Fold ¼ inch of the raw edge to the inside of the skirt, pin, and baste all around. Then top-stitch near the folded edge. Be careful not to catch any of the pastel material as you are hemming the white layer. Next, fold the white fabric up on the inside, bringing the stitched edge to just meet the lower lace seam *(Fig. 19)*. Pin the hem in place, and, using small stitches, slip-stitch the hem of the white dress. Press the hem flat.

22

Repeat the hemming on the pastel underslip, folding the final hem up about ¼ inch more than the white dress. This will make the underslip slightly shorter than the overdress.

23

If you wish to trim the white layer with an edging of lace, pin a length of lace to the hemmed bottom, beginning at the center back. Clip the lace leaving ¼ inch excess at both ends. Turn under the excess and machine-sew the lace to the edge close to the bottom. To finish the dress properly you must add a flower trim. Directions for making the flowers follow.

FLOWER TRIM

The lace used on the dress in this book had a very geometric, formal pattern that lent itself to an alternating flower-bow-flower decorative pattern. More than likely, your lace will be different—so you might wish to do several clusters of flowers instead, each with a bow. Or perhaps you might decide on one large group of flowers and bows in the front of the dress, leaving the rest of the lace border plain. Let the lace "speak" to you as to how best to arrange the flowers and ribbon trimming. Just remember that you should sew any decoration only to the white layer and leave the pastel slip free.

MATERIALS NEEDED

(for a single flower)

1 piece medium-weight Pellon, about 1 x 1 inch

9 inches of pale green rayon seam tape, cut into four 2¼-inch lengths

3 or 4 stamens, double-edged type (available from craft stores in assorted colors)

6 inches of white rayon seam tape

1 inch of pale lilac rayon seam tape

1 piece of pale yellow felt, about ½ x ½ inch

1 self-shank pearl dome button, about ¼ inch in diameter

4 inches of ribbon for a bow, ⅛ inch wide

Sewing needle

Threads to match

Note: The pattern you decide on will determine the number of flowers you will need, and in turn the amount of seam tape, buttons, Pellon and so forth.

1

Make a circle on the Pellon by tracing around a ten-cent piece. Cut out the circle and put it aside.

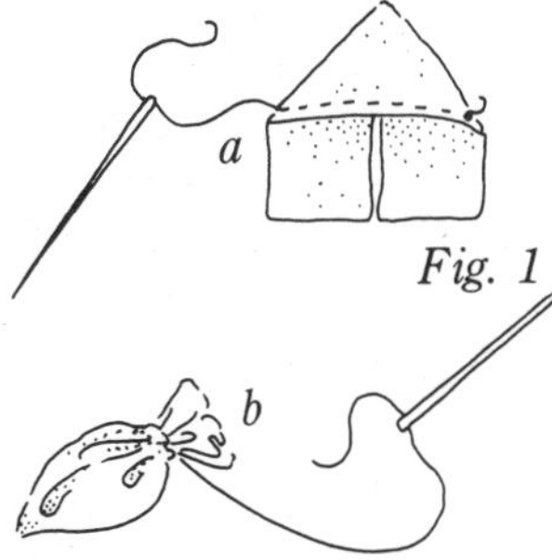

Fig. 1

2

Start with the 4 lengths of pale green seam tape. These will form the leaves of your flower. Fold the tape as shown in *Fig. 1a*. Run a gathering stitch along the straight edge of the folded tape, as illustrated. Holding the 2 tabs at the bottom, pull the gathering thread as tightly as you can and then wrap the thread around the gathered tape at its base *(Fig. 1b)*. Whip-stitch several times to lock the wrapped thread in place. This is the bottom of the leaf. Leave a length of thread dangling. Put the leaf aside. Repeat this process to make 3 more leaves. Use the extra thread to attach the leaves to the Pellon disc, 2 on each side.

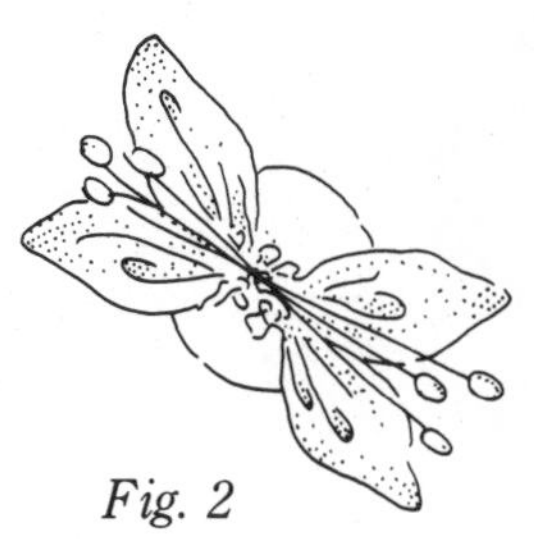

Fig. 2

3

Place 3 or 4 of the stamens on top of the Pellon disc and open out to make a fan shape on each side. Sew the stamens to the center of the Pellon *(Fig. 2)*.

4

Using a tiny stitch and seam allowance, French-seam the 2 ends of the 6-inch length of white seam tape together, forming a ring. Run a gathering thread all around one edge *(Fig. 3a)*, pulling the thread so that the ring is gathered into a disc *(Fig. 3b)*. Leave a small opening in the center. Lock the gathering in place with a couple of whip stitches. Place the gathered-tape disc on top of the Pellon disc, centering it so that the seam is on the bottom. Stitch it to the Pellon.

Fig. 3

5

Take the 1-inch length of lilac tape and fold it in half lengthwise. Make a crease on the fold, open the tape out, and sew a gathering stitch through the crease line. Gather the tape tightly and whip-stitch it to lock. Place this piece right in the center of the disc opening, on top of the stitched-down stamens, and sew it through the opening to the Pellon *(Fig. 4)*.

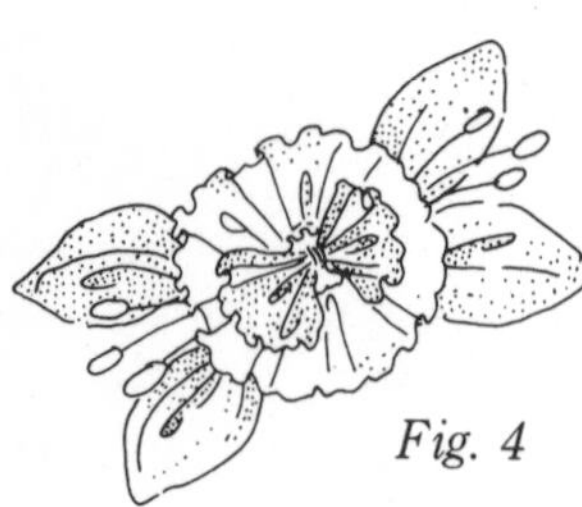

Fig. 4

6

From the yellow felt cut out a circle slightly larger than your pearl button. Center it on the gathered center of the lilac tape so that it covers the center opening of the white disc and run several stitches through the felt to the Pellon base. Bring the needle and thread back up to the felt side, slip the button onto the needle, and sew it securely through the yellow felt to the Pellon base *(Fig. 5)*. On the Pellon side, lock-stitch and clip the thread.

Fig. 5

7

Ravel the threads of the lilac tape so that it becomes feathery and looks a little like stamens. Now the flower is complete *(Fig. 6)*.

Fig. 6

8

To attach the flower to the dress, stitch it to the lace by slip-stitching only the Pellon base all around. Do not stitch through to the pastel under layer. No stitching will show on the flower itself. Alternate flowers with ribbon bows to make a lovely trim.

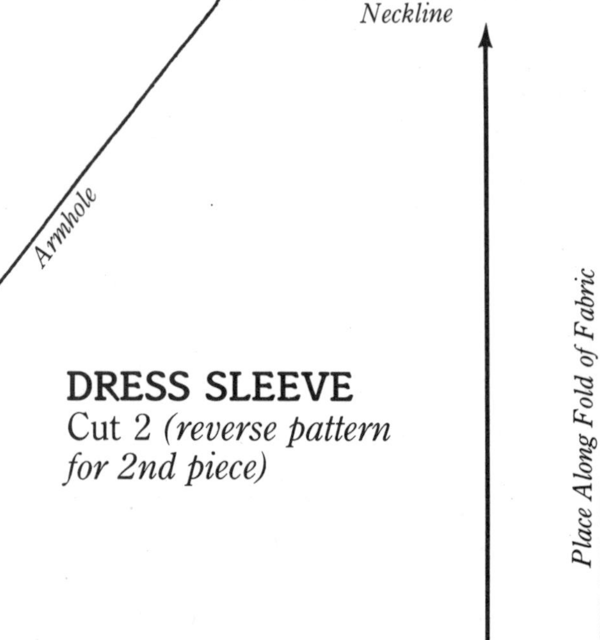

BABY'S EVERYDAY DRESS

Baby's everyday dress is a short untrimmed version of the presentation gown, without the front placket, the lace and flower trim and bottom section. Use the sleeve pattern on page 84.

MATERIALS NEEDED

Printed cotton fabric, 12 x 36 inches
Contrasting fabric, 5 x 19 inches
12 inches of bias tape in same contrasting color
Small hook and bar
Sewing needle
Threads to match

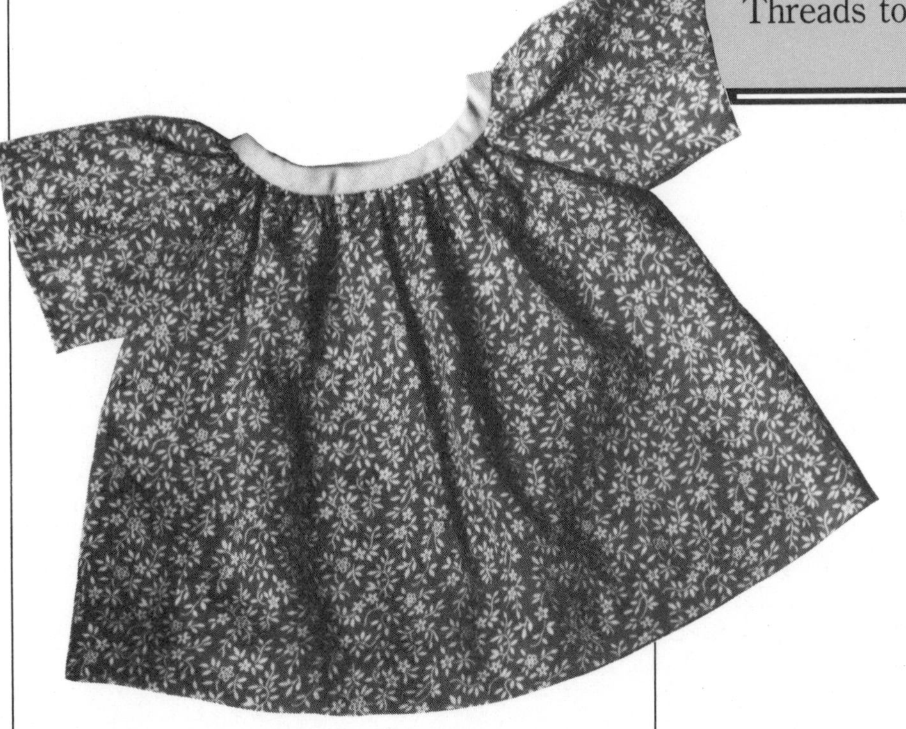

1

Following the directions on page 24, trace the sleeve pattern from the book and cut it out.

2

Lay the printed fabric on your work surface and smooth it out. From this fabric cut:

1 dress piece 9½ x 26 inches
2 sleeve pieces, using the tissue pattern

3

Use the sleeve pattern to cut out 2 sleeve pieces from the contrasting fabric.

4

With the wrong side facing out, pin, then machine-sew the side seams of each sleeve piece together, leaving a ¼-inch seam allowance. Press the seams open and join the outer sleeve pieces to their linings, right sides in, and stitch together *(Fig. 1)* Put aside.

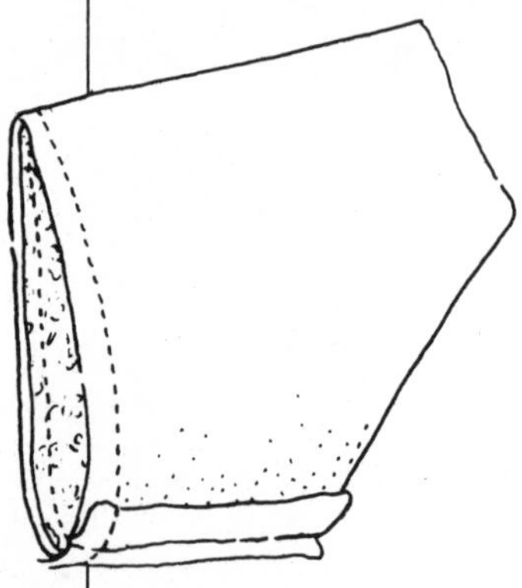

Fig. 1

5

Measure 6½ inches down from the top of one short edge of the dress piece, and mark. With the wrong side facing out, machine-sew the back seam of the dress from that point to the bottom edge, leaving a 1-inch seam allowance. Finish off the seam edges.

6

Following the measurements in step 11 on page 80, cut out the armholes from the dress. With the wrong side of the dress still facing out, set the sleeves (right side out) into the dress, pinning them all around (step 14, page 81). Machine-sew the sleeves into place. Turn the dress right side out.

7

Run a gathering stitch all around the dress neckline, gathering the neckline until it measures 10½ inches. Following step 17, stitch the bias tape to the outside of the neckline according to the instructions on the package of bias tape, leaving ½ inch extra tape at both ends *(Fig.2)*. Finish off the neckline as in step 18. Add a hook and bar to the neckline.

8

Turn the dress wrong side out. Pin up ¼ inch of fabric all around the hem edge and top-stitch in place. Next, turn that edge up ¾ inch and hem by hand. Press the hem flat, then turn the dress right side out. If you wish, add a bow at the neck edge, or maybe some tiny buttons down the front, or even a touch of lace.

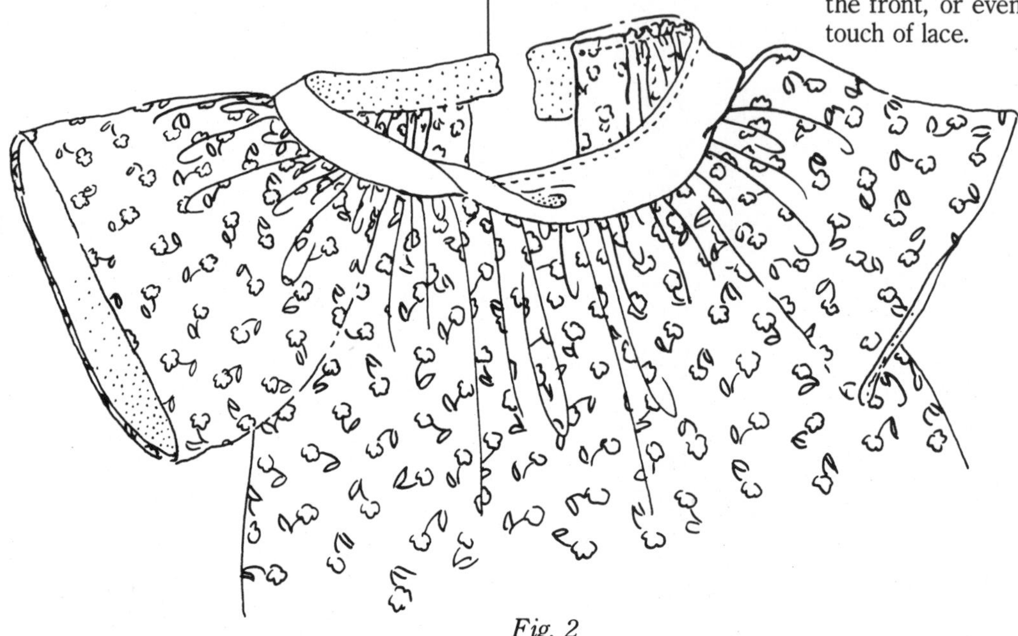

Fig. 2

TEDDY BEAR ACCESSORIES

Papa's Flower Book

Mama's Needlepoint

Baby's Yo-Yo Blanket

Baby's Rag Doll Bear

Living with Your Bears

PAPA'S FLOWER BOOK

Papa likes to keep his book of pressed flowers at his side at all times. If you wish, you could use a small notebook covered in a colored paper, and in place of real pressed flowers, pictures could be cut out of magazines and catalogs and glued in the book. If, on the other hand, you wish to make your very own little volume, the following instructions will show you how to go about it. The pattern begins on page 92.

MATERIALS NEEDED

1 sheet of medium-weight cardboard, 9 x 12 inches

Rice paper or bond typing paper, to make approximately 30 sheets, 3½-x-4½-inches

Three different colored papers, such as construction paper, gift wrap or fancy paper of your choice, approximately 9 x 12 inches

6 inches of ribbon, ⅛ inch wide

White glue

Metal-edge ruler

Single-edge razor blades

Waxed paper

1

Following the directions on page 24, trace the pattern pieces from the book, then transfer them to oaktag. Cut the pieces out.

2

On medium-weight cardboard trace 2 binder boards (#1) and 1 spine (#2). Set aside. From the rice or typing paper cut out approximately 30 full-size book pages using pattern piece #8 and 15 partial pages using pattern piece #9. *Note:* The use of the partial page gives the book its correct thickness at the spine and at the same time cuts down on the bulk.

3

From your 3 different sheets of colored paper:
Color 1: cut 2
 cover papers (#3)
Color 2: cut 1
 spine paper (#4)
 and 4 book corners (#5)
Color 3: cut 2
 endpapers (#6)
 and 1 label (#7)
Note: If you have chosen a paper with a directional pattern for the cover, remember to reverse the pattern when cutting out the back cover.

4

Glue the cover papers to the cardboard binders, folding the ½-inch allowance on the 3 sides to the inside *(Fig. 1)*. Cover with waxed paper, place a weight on top and leave overnight to dry (8 hours, to be safe). These will now be the front and back covers of the book.

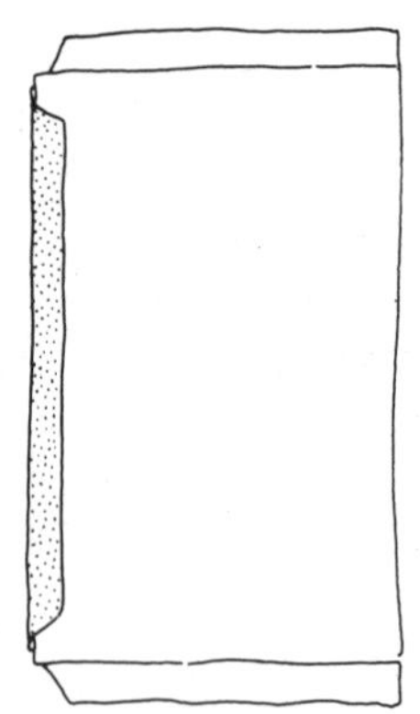

Fig. 1

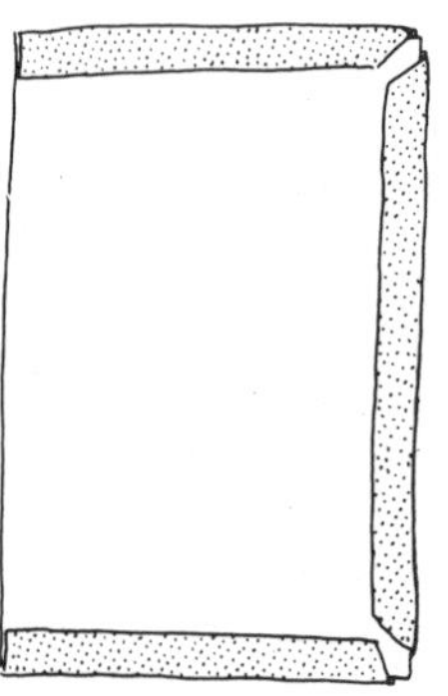

5

Take 4 sheets of full-size book pages and glue them together along one long edge, as indicated on the pattern (#8). Put aside and repeat with 4 more sheets. Weight down and allow to dry, again overnight. These 2 sets form the first and last 4 sheets of your book.

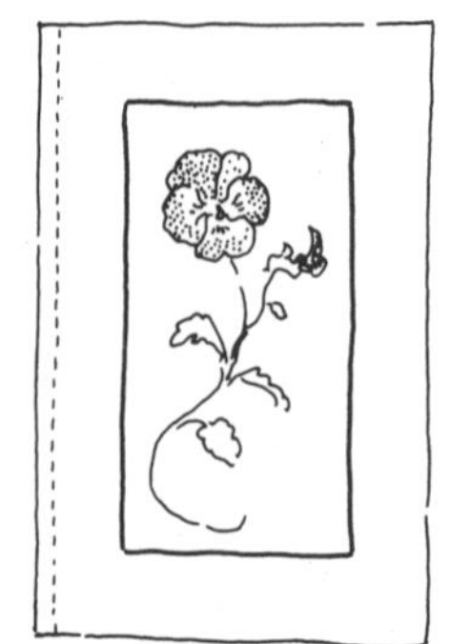

Fig. 2

6

Divide the remaining full sheets in 2 piles. Set 1 pile aside. Taking 1 sheet at a time from the remaining pile and following the placement on the pattern (#8), trace around the stencil (#10) with a thick felt-tip pen. This will form a frame in which you will later glue your flowers *(Fig. 2)*.

7

Take 1 preglued group of 4 sheets (step 5) and place them on your work surface. These are the last 4 sheets of your book. On top of this group, glue 1 stenciled page, next a partial sheet, and then a blank sheet (where you will write the flower's name) *(Fig. 3)*. Repeat this process, building up to the ⅜-inch thickness of the spine. You should end with a partial sheet before adding the second group of 4 preglued sheets. When complete, add a heavy weight and leave the book to dry overnight.

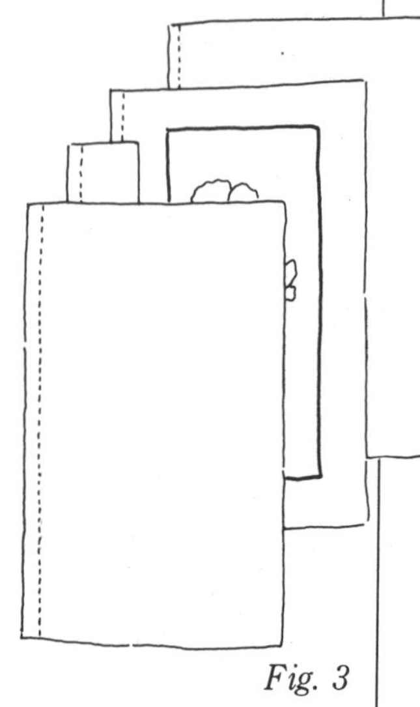

Fig. 3

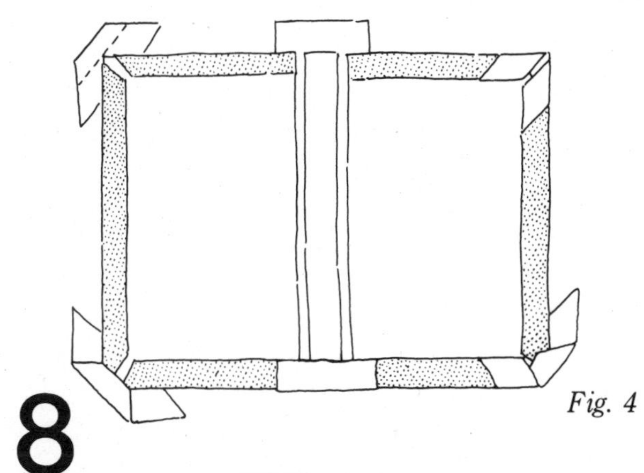

Fig. 4

8

While the pages are drying, you may continue working on the covers if they have dried. Following *Fig. 4*, glue the corner pieces to the front and back covers; fold the excess to the inside of the cover and glue down. Next, place the spine paper on your work surface, wrong side up. The paper is divided into 3 sections. The outer sections are marked *A*, the inner is marked *B*. Coat one spine paper section *A* with glue. Place a cover on it, right side down, matching *A* on the cover with *A* on the spine paper, and glue down. Then glue the spine board (#2) down along section *B* of the spine paper. Coat the remaining spine paper *A* section with glue and add the second cover. Make sure all top and bottom edges align. Fold the excess spine paper down and glue to the inside. Cover this completed casing with waxed paper, weight it down and leave it to dry.

Fig. 5

9

Fold the 2 endpapers in half, 1 for the front of the book and 1 for the back. Cut 2 sheets of waxed paper a good 1 to 2 inches larger than the book sheets. Place your glued-together pages on your work surface, with the first page facing up. Slip 1 sheet of waxed paper under the first page. This will catch any excess glue. Cover the top surface of this page with a thin coating of glue. On top of this glued page, place 1 of the folded endpapers, folded side flush with the long edge of the preglued page *(Fig. 5)*. With a paper towel press the paper flat. Turn the book to the other side and repeat the process of gluing the second endpaper in place.

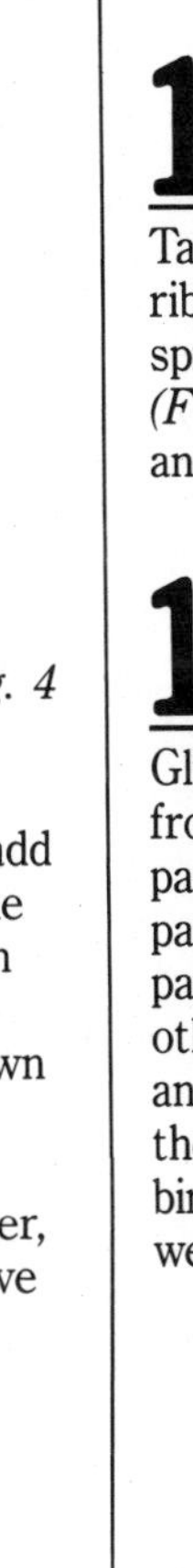

10

Take the 6-inch length of ribbon and glue it to the spine of the book pages *(Fig. 6)*. Add a weight and dry overnight.

11

Glue the label on the front cover as shown on pattern #3. Slip waxed paper between the end papers and glue the other half of the front and back endpapers to the inside of the cover binders *(Fig. 7)*. Add a weight and dry.

Fig. 6

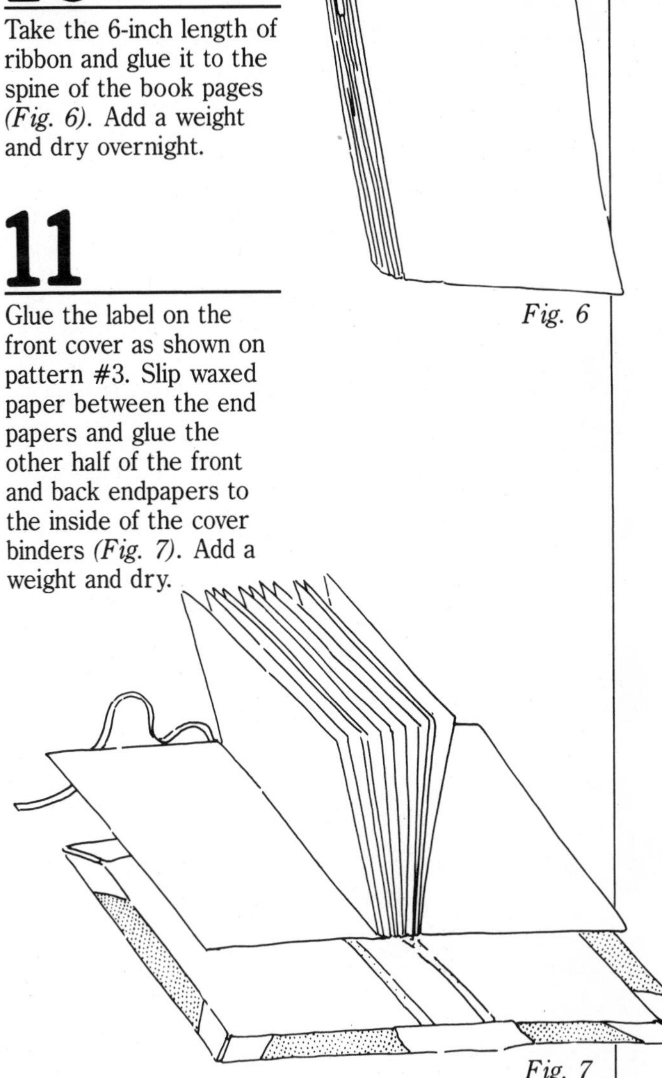

Fig. 7

12

When the book is completely dry, pull the ribbon marker down into the book pages. You are now ready to glue in your dried flowers or flower prints as you acquire them. The name of each blossom can be written on the full page preceding the flower.

PAPA'S FLOWER BOOK PATTERN

#2

SPINE

#1 BINDER BOARD

#10
OUTLINE
STENCIL

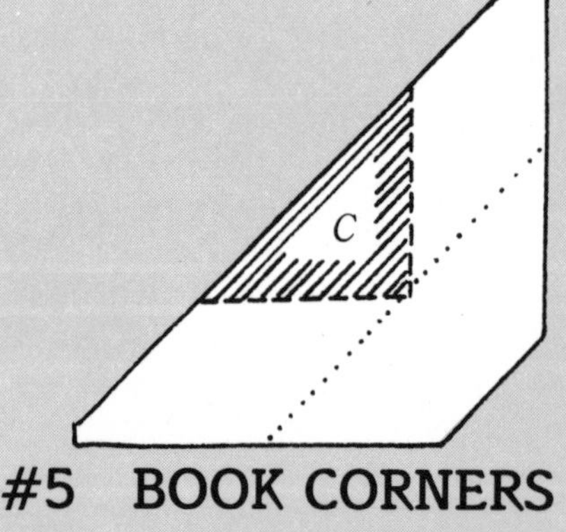

#5 BOOK CORNERS

SPINE PAPER

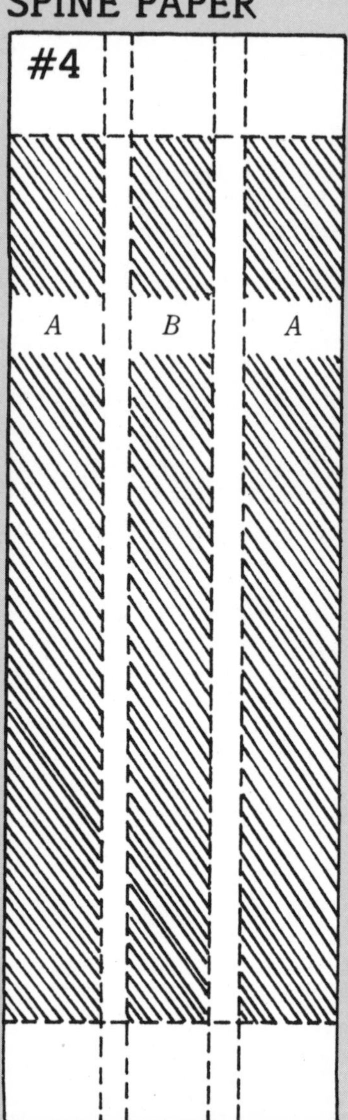

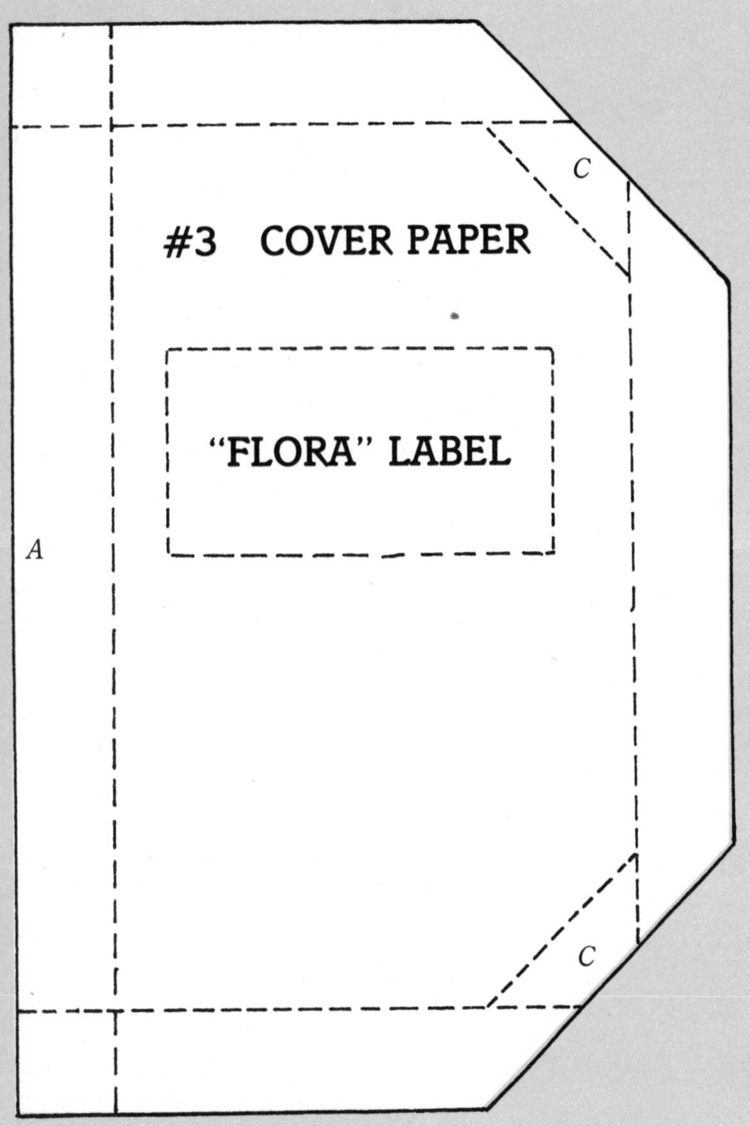
#3 COVER PAPER
"FLORA" LABEL
A
C
C

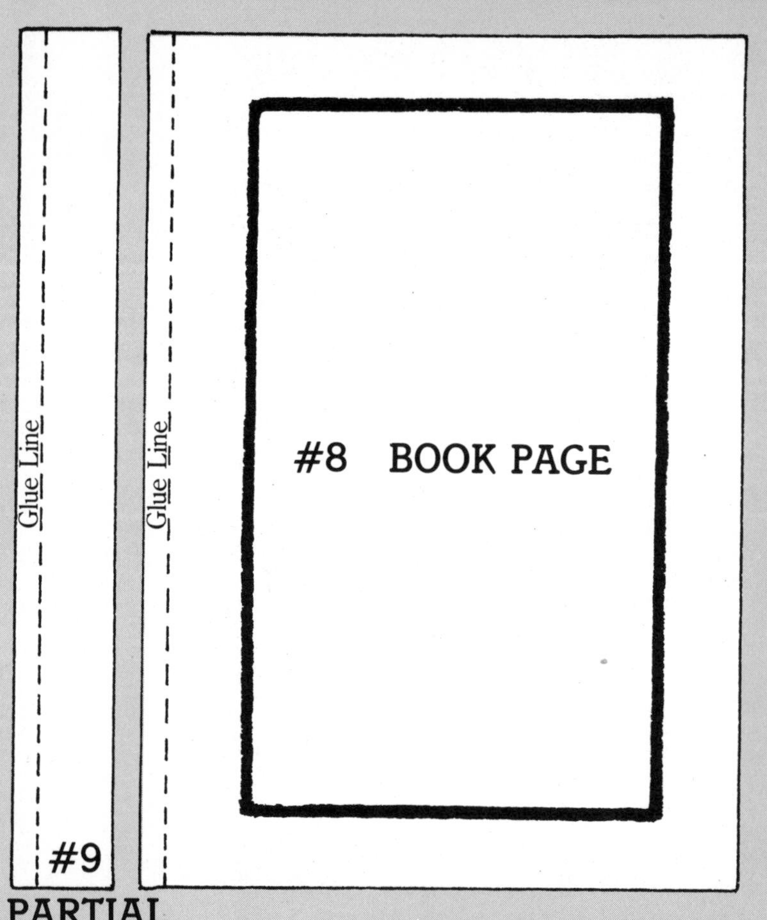

PARTIAL PAGE

#7 LABEL

#6 ENDPAPERS

MAMA'S NEEDLEPOINT

Mama's Teddy Bear needlepoint design is worked in two easy stitches: the body of the canvas is done in a tent stitch and the border in a straight gobelin. Both are illustrated in the Stitch Dictionary on page 14. The canvas used has 10 mesh to the inch and the yarns are 3-ply Persian. The needlepoint design is 37 squares wide by 48 squares long. The diagram is drawn so that 1 square equals 1 stitch and each color has its own symbol.

MATERIALS NEEDED

Canvas: 10 mesh to the inch, about 6 x 7 inches

Yarns: 1 skein for each color except the background, for which you will need 2 skeins (see below for color chart)

Tapestry needle with a blunt end and an eye large enough to accommodate the yarn—no larger

Masking tape, 1 inch wide

1

Before beginning, bind the raw edges of your canvas with masking tape so that it will not unravel as you work.

2

Since you will be working on a blank piece of canvas and must count all the stitches, it would be wise to start with the bear. He is the most difficult part of the work. First mark the center of the canvas. Checking the illustration, opposite, start working your stitches at the bear's waistline and continue working down to finish both legs.

3

Again starting at the waist, work up until the bear is complete. Next, do the stems and flowers and then the letters.

4

When you are ready to fill in the background, start in the upper right corner and fill in with the tent stitch.

5

The last area to work on the needlepoint is the border. When you are finished, the canvas should be blocked. Since this is a small piece, it will not have been too greatly stretched out of shape. Place a terry-cloth towel on your ironing board. Place the needlepoint face down on the towel and start pinning down one long side, using T-pins and a ruler as a guide. Make certain that it is pinned straight. Now pin across the top, again checking that the canvas is straight. Continue pinning the remaining 2 sides. When it is perfectly straight and square and pinned securely, place a damp cloth over the canvas and steam well. Do not press your iron down, but rather let it slide across the surface of the material. Continue to steam the needlepoint until it lies flat and smooth. Leave it to dry overnight.

COLOR CHART

Symbol	Area	Color
/	Background	Pale beige
X	Border	Beige
•	Lettering	Brick red
o	Border corners & neck ribbon	Pale blue
C	Flower stems & leaves	Pale green
V	Flower center	Yellow
////	Eyes & nose	Black
U	Bear	Medium tan
(blank)	Flower petals	White

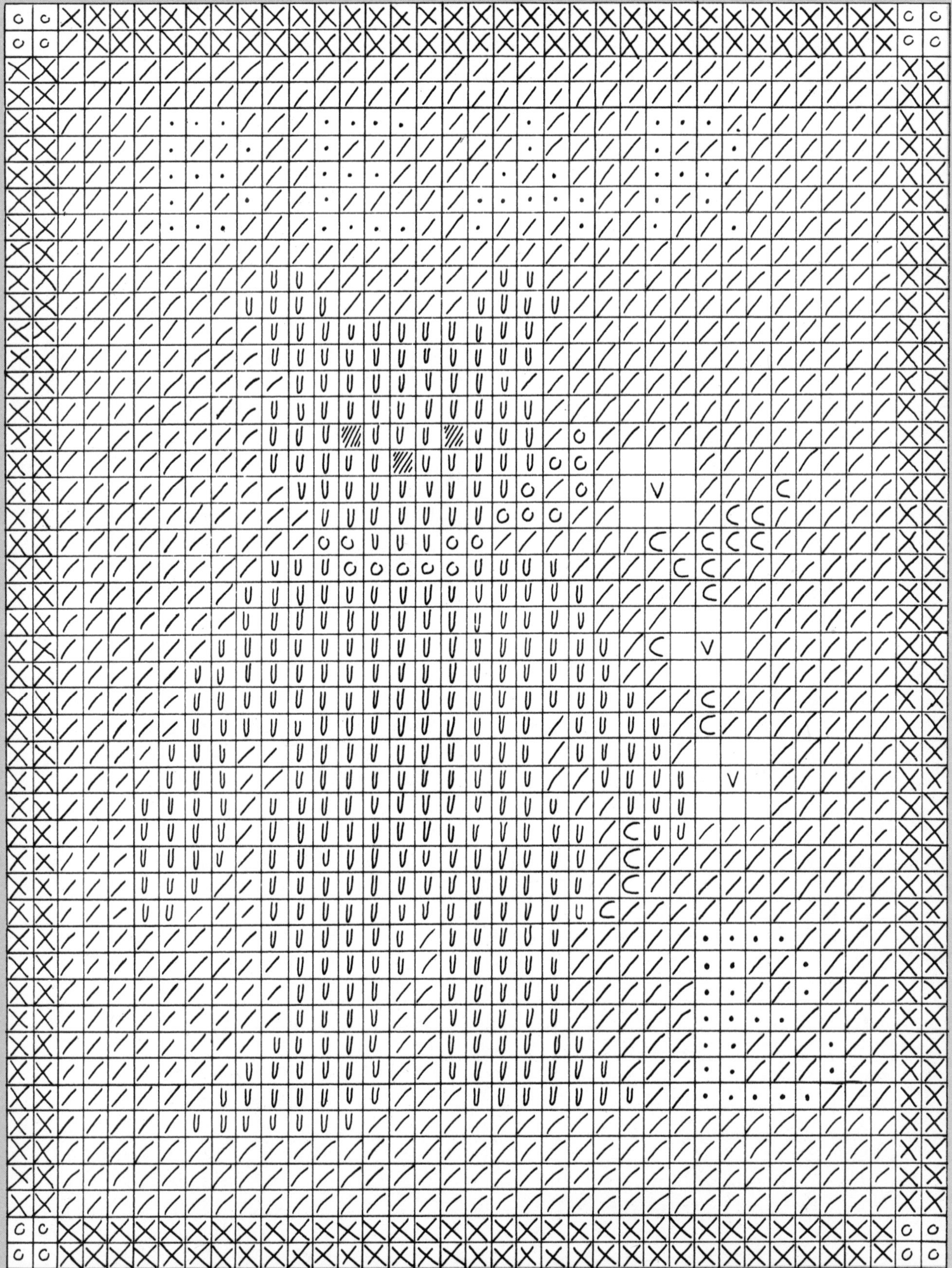

BABY'S YO-YO BLANKET

Yo-yos are a nice change from patchwork and make up into wonderful blankets for real babies as well as Teddy Bears.

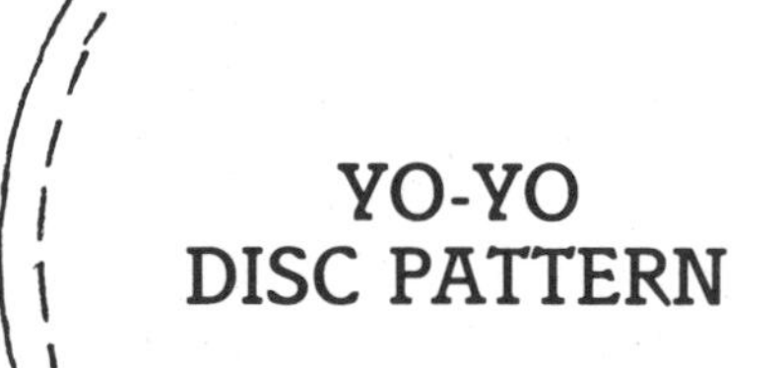

MATERIALS NEEDED

- Color *A*: thin cotton fabric, 9 x 36 inches
- Color *B*: thin cotton fabric, 9 x 36 inches
- Color *C*: thin cotton fabric, 9 x 36 inches
- 1⅓ yards of double-fold bias tape to match fabric *C* (optional)
- 2 yards of Cluny lace, 1 inch wide (optional)
- 8 inches of ribbon to match fabric *C*, ¼ inch wide (optional)
- Threads to match

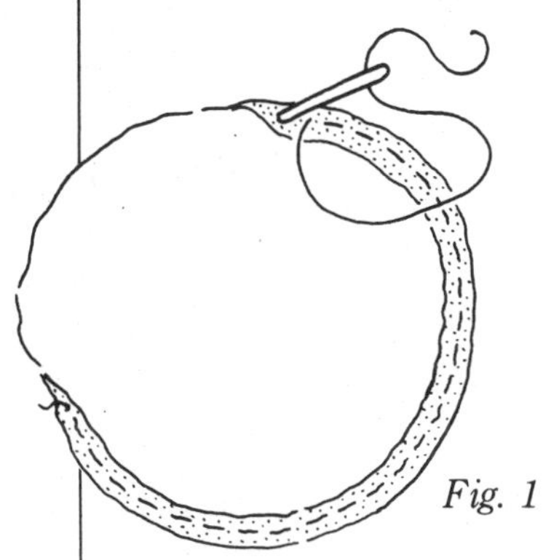
Fig. 1

1

Following the directions on page 24, trace the yo-yo disc pattern below from the book, then transfer the tracing onto oaktag or thin cardboard.

2

Trace 15 circles on the wrong side of fabric color *A*. Cut them out. Trace and cut out 20 circles from fabric color *B* and 28 from fabric color *C*.

3

Start with the circles of color *A*. Take 1 circle, wrong side up, and folding the edge of the disc over ⅛ inch as you go, run a gathering stitch (use double thread) through the folded-over edge all the way around the circle *(Fig. 1)*. As you stitch, carefully pull the gathering thread so the fabric pulls in over itself; when the yo-yo is completed, this will form a small open circle at the center of the disc *(Fig. 2)*. Back-stitch to lock the gather, and clip off the excess thread. Flatten out the gathered circle so that it forms a flat, round disc with the small opening in its center. Set aside and continue until all color *A* circles are completed.

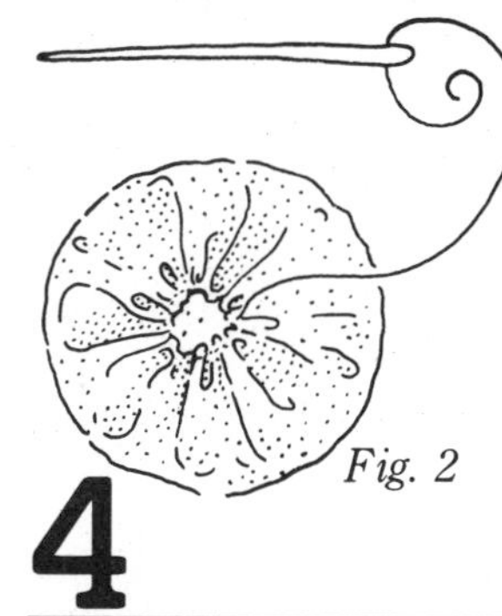
Fig. 2

4

Take 2 discs, placing one on top of the other with the openings facing in. Stitching at the very edge of the discs, whip-stitch 2 together using 5 or 6 small stitches to create a hinge *(Fig. 3)*.

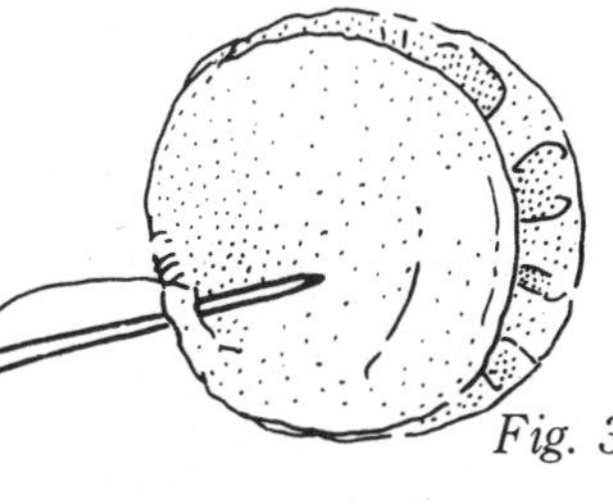

Fig. 3

Lock-stitch and clip the thread. Open them out so the 2 openings are now facing up. Place another disc on top of one of these, opening facing down, and again whip the disc edges together, lock-stich, and clip the thread. Open out and set aside *(Fig. 4)*.

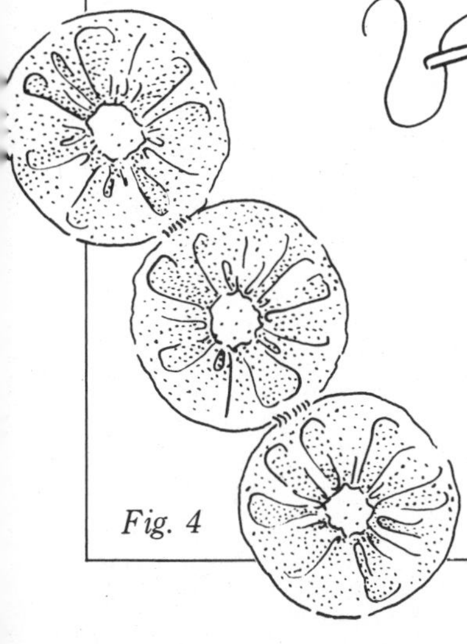

Fig. 4

5

Take 3 more yo-yos and stitch them together as you did with the first 3. Continue working in sets of 3 until you have stitched together 5 sets of 3 yo-yos each.

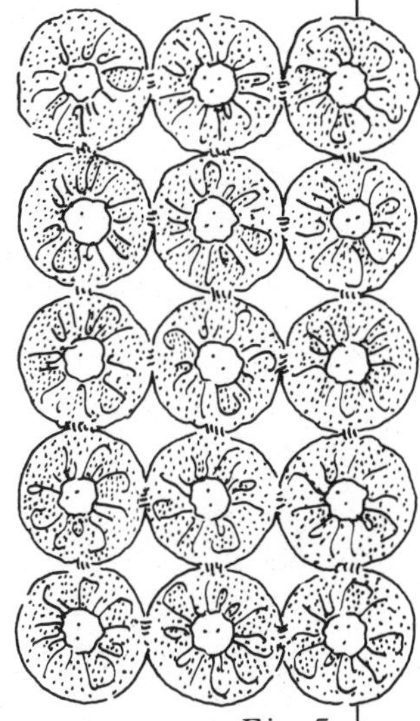
Fig. 5

6

Take 2 sets of 3 yo-yos, placing one exactly on top of the other with the openings facing in. Whip-stitch the first 2 circles together, then the second 2 and finally the third 2. Open out so that all the circles are facing up. You should have a piece 2 yo-yos by 3 yo-yos. Place another set of 3 on top of a stitched row of 3, with the openings facing down. Sew these together as before, and continue joining the rows until all 5 are joined in one piece measuring 3 yo-yos by 5 yo-yos *(Fig. 5)*.

7

You are now ready to make the yo-yos from color *B*. Do this exactly as you did with color *A*. When all 20 are completed, take 5 of them and whip-stitch a row together, forming hinges as you did with the color *A* yo-yos. When this row is finished, set it aside and continue with another row of 5. Continue until you have 4 separate rows of 5 yo-yos each.

8

Place the completed color *A* yo-yo piece on your work surface, openings facing up. Take a strip of color *B* yo-yos and place them, openings facing down, on top of a row of 5 *A* yo-yos. Whip-stitch each *B* yo-yo to an *A* yo-yo. With a second strip of *B* yo-yos, repeat this on the opposite long side of the *A* piece. Open out the strips. Sew a strip of *B* yo-yos to each of the other sides of the piece. Now you have a piece measuring 5 yo-yos by 7 yo-yos, with color *B* forming a border *(Fig. 6)*.

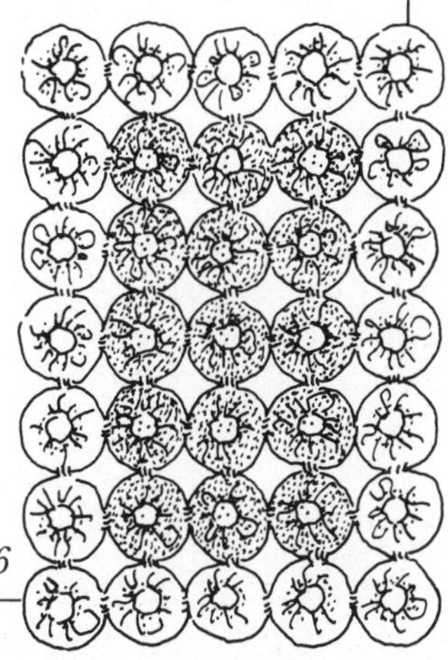
Fig. 6

9

Make up the 28 yo-yos of color *C* as you did with the others. Whip-stitch together 4 rows of 7 yo-yos each. Place the completed *A-B* piece on your work surface, openings up, and as you did in step 8, attach a strip of *C* yo-yos to each side of the large piece, giving you a blanket measuring 7 yo-yos by 9 yo-yos, with color *C* forming the outside border. The body of the blanket is now completed, and can very well be used as it is.

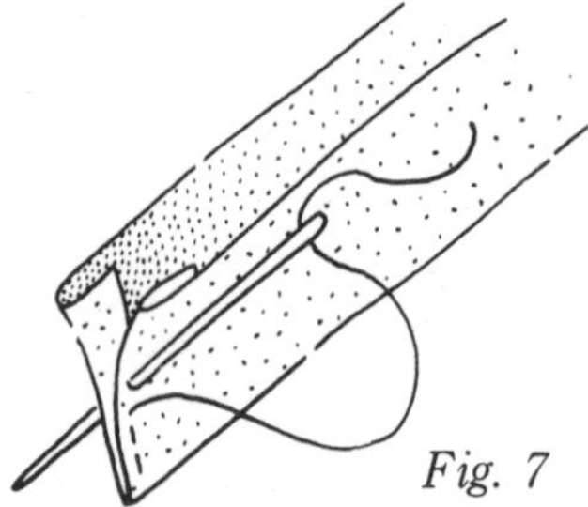
Fig. 7

10

If you wish to add trimming, take the prefolded bias tape and open up one end. Tuck about ¼ inch of the bias inside and stitch the end closed *(Fig. 7)*.

Fig. 8

11

Place the blanket, openings up, on your work surface, and starting at the bottom center yo-yo (the row of 7), place the bias tape on top of the edge of the blanket so the folded edge of the tape lines up with the bottom edge of the yo-yo. Stitch the binding to the yo-yo. Ease the tape along the edge to the next yo-yo and again stitch *(Fig. 8)*.

12

Continue stitching to the last yo-yo on that row. Whip-stitch the binding to the center of the last yo-yo to lock. Now make 13 or 14 small gathering stitches through the binding. Pull the thread and tighten the gathers until the gathered edge curves to match the curve of the corner yo-yo. This should position the binding so you can now work up the next side *(Fig. 9)*. Do not stitch the gathered section to the yo-yos yet.

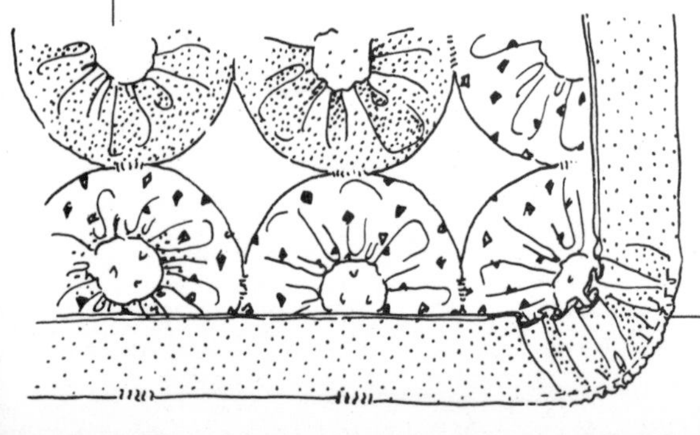
Fig. 9

13

Continue this process all around the blanket. When you are back to your starting point, trim any excess binding, leaving ¼ inch extra. Open the cut end and fold in the ¼ inch of tape. Whip together the binding ends. Finally whip together the binding and the yo-yos at the four gathered corners. Open the binding out.

Fig. 10

14

Again starting at the bottom center, whip-stitch the Cluny lace to the binding, the straight edge of the lacing lining up with the unsewn (double) binding edge. Make sure to catch both edges of the binding as you stitch the lace to it. When you reach the corners, loosely ease in the lace so that it will not pull when opened out *(Fig. 10)*. The lace should also look slightly gathered.

15

Continue whip-stitching the lace all around the binding, using small stitches, until you are back where you started. Neatly whip-stitch the two raw ends of lace together wrong side up. Open the lace out.

16

Steam-iron the blanket wrong side up—but do not press it flat. While the blanket is drying, make a bow with the ribbon. Sew it to the right side of the blanket at the bottom end, so it covers the binding seam. Your blanket is completed.

BABY'S RAG DOLL BEAR

Everyone should have a bear doll—even a Teddy Bear. This is Baby Bear's favorite toy. It was constructed from a medium-weight woven fabric. The pattern is on page 104.

MATERIALS NEEDED

- Medium-weight fabric, 8 x 18 inches
- 1 dome button, ⅝-inch diameter
- 2 black buttons, ¼-inch diameter
- 4 pearl shirt buttons
- Stuffing (left over from making Teddy Bears)
- Black embroidery thread
- Scrap of black felt
- 10 inches of ribbon, ¼ inch wide (optional)
- 14 inches of double-edged white eyelet, 2 x 14 inches (optional)
- White glue
- Straight pins
- T-pins
- Sewing needles, various lengths
- Carpet or button thread to match
- Mercerized thread to match

1

Following the directions on page 24, trace the doll pattern pieces from the book. Transfer them to oaktag and cut them out.

2

Lay the fabric on your work surface and smooth it out. Turn up the corner of one end *(Fig. 1)*. Place, then pin the head and nose pieces on the single-layer area of the fabric. Cut out 1 of each. Place the straight edge of the arm and leg patterns on the folded bias edge and cut out 2 of each. Place the body pattern on the doubled fabric, away from the folded edge, and cut out 2 separate pieces. Take a small piece of fabric, fold it in half right side out (not on the bias), and place the straight edge of the ear pattern on the fold *(Fig. 2)*. Cut out 2 ears.

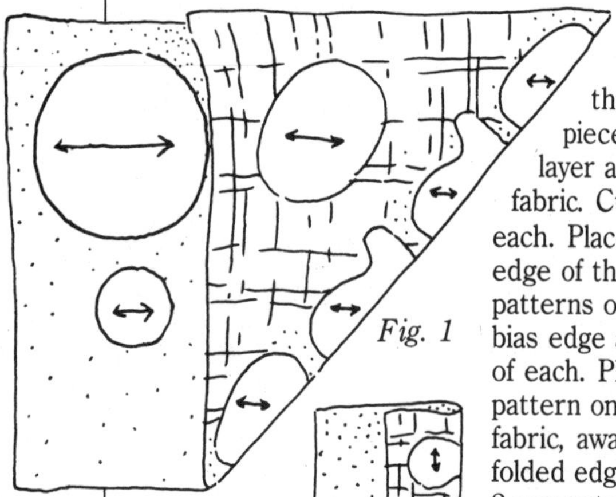

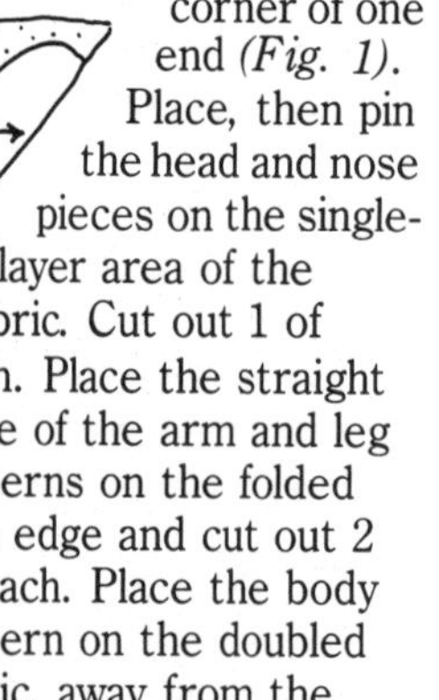

Fig. 1

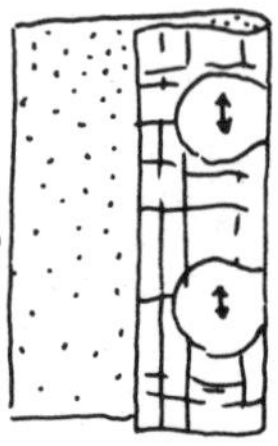

Fig. 2

3

Using carpet thread, run a gathering stitch all around the edge of the small (nose) circle, wrong side up. Do not clip the thread. Place a thin layer of stuffing on the wrong side of the fabric, keeping it smooth and even in thickness. Trim the stuffing to be slightly smaller than the fabric circle.

4

Cover the top of the dome button with a little glue and place the glued dome side on the center of the stuffing-covered nose circle *(Fig. 3)*. Carefully pull the gathering thread until the fabric encloses the button and the raw edges are on the under side of the button. Tie the thread and then stitch back and forth from one side to the other to secure the raw edges of the fabric. Knot the thread and set the button aside *(Fig. 5)*.

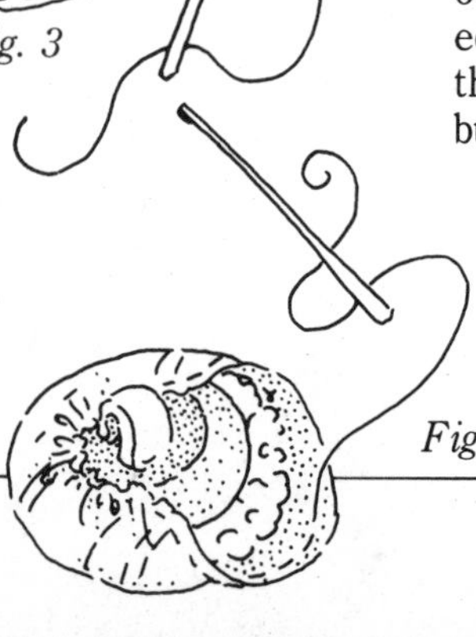

Fig. 3

Fig. 4

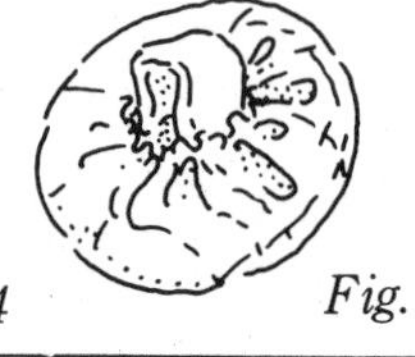

Fig. 5

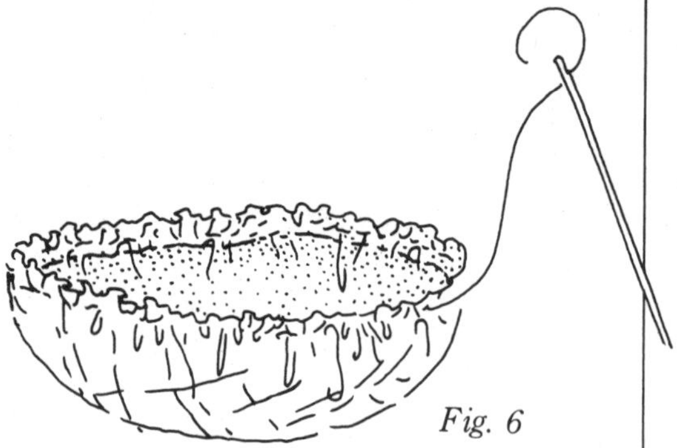

Fig. 6

5

Take the large (head) circle and, folding under ⅛ inch as you go, run a gathering stitch as you did with the yo-yos (step 3, page 99). When complete, gather slightly so that the circle forms a kind of bowl shape, right side out *(Fig. 6)*. Do not clip the thread. Start filling with small wads of stuffing and continue pulling the gathering thread as it fills and starts to form a ball shape. Gather just until the opening is slightly smaller than the base of the fabric-covered button. Lock your gathering thread and continue to stuff until you have a nice firm ball, working the stuffing through the opening with a knitting needle.

6

When you have finished stuffing the ball, place it on your work surface with the opening facing up. Place the fabric-covered dome button, dome side up, over the opening and pin it in place with T-pins *(Fig. 7)*. Slip-stitch the button to the ball securely. Now you have a head and muzzle.

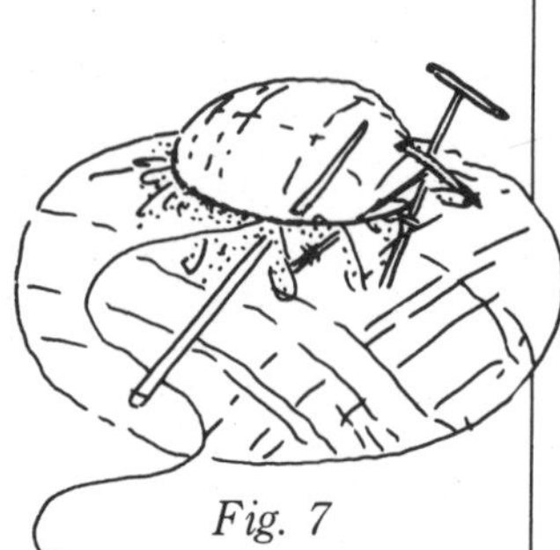

Fig. 7

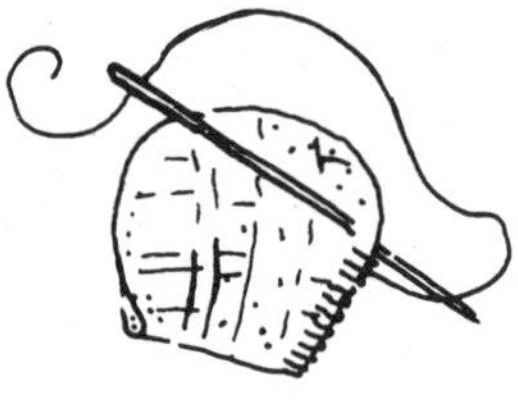

Fig. 8

7

Take one ear and pin it closed, right side out. Using a small buttonhole stitch, work from one side of the raw edge to the other *(Fig. 8)*. When finished, lock-stitch. Position the ear and sew it to the head with slip stitches. Repeat this with the second ear.

8

Using the directions on page 40 as a guide, sew on the 2 black buttons to form the eyes. To make the mouth, use embroidery thread and follow the directions for the Teddy Bears' mouth, page 39. Then glue on the black felt nose *(Fig. 9)*, which will cover the knots of the embroidery thread.

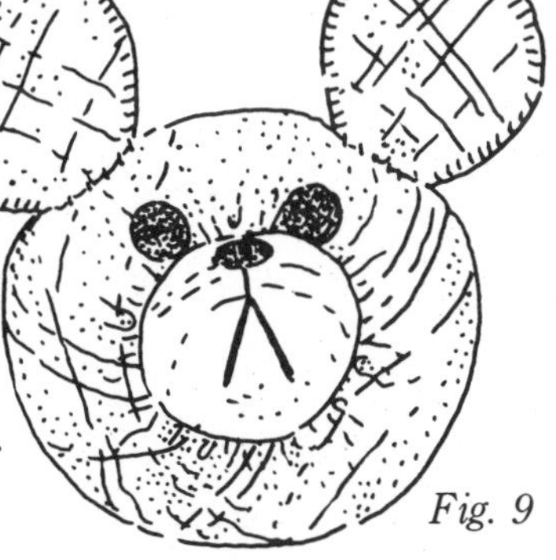

Fig. 9

9

Machine-stitch the arm and leg pieces together, still folded wrong side out, as far as the *X* marks, leaving a ⅛-inch seam allowance. Sew together the 2 body pieces, wrong side out, from the *X* mark around to the second *X* mark, leaving a ⅛-inch seam allowance. Turn the body right side out, and trim the seam allowance at the curves if necessary.

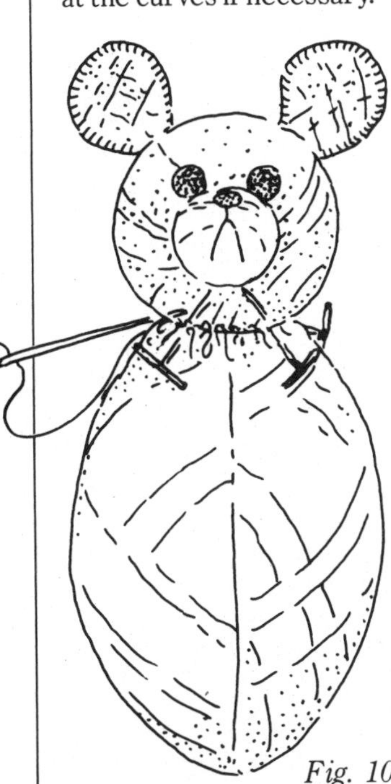

Fig. 10

10

Take the body, and at the open end fold under ⅛ inch of fabric. Run a double gathering thread around this edge. Do not clip the thread. This is the bear's neck. Stuff the body until it is nice and firm. Pull the gathering thread, adding more stuffing if necessary to make the neck area firm. Continue pulling until the neck is almost closed, and tie off. Place the bottom of the head over the neck opening. Pin the head to the body with T-pins *(Fig. 10)*, then slip-stitch it in place. The head and body now form one piece.

11

Stuff the arms and legs, but not too firmly. Fold in the raw edges of each limb and slip-stitch the openings closed.

12

Using a long needle and double thread, stitch a button to the outside of one arm at the shoulder. (The arm seam should be at the back.) Lock-stitch on the inner side of the arm and then run the needle through the shoulder area of the body, as marked on the pattern. Bring the needle right through the body and out where the mark is at the opposite shoulder area. Run the needle through the second arm and pull the thread tight, so that both arms are taut against the body. Back-stitch 2 or 3 times to lock, and with the same thread, add a button to that arm *(Fig. 11)*. Again, back-stitch.

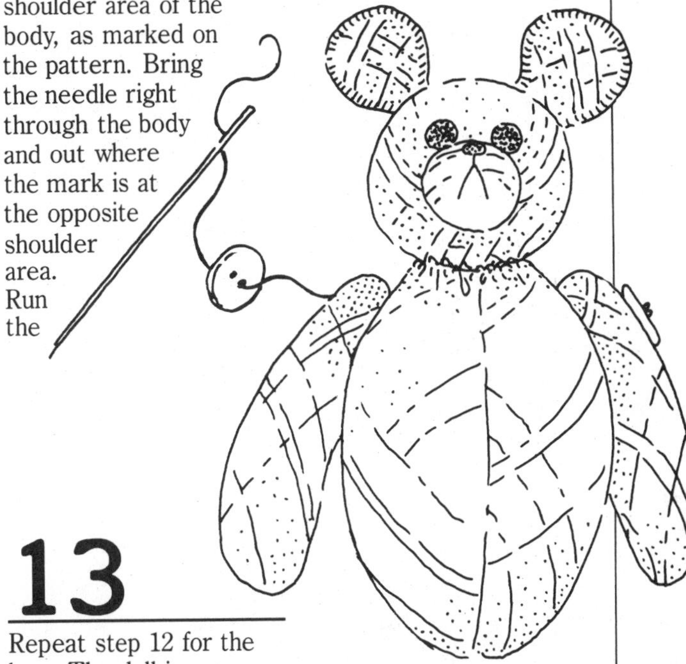

Fig. 11

13

Repeat step 12 for the legs. The doll is now complete.

14

To make the bear doll's collar, French-seam the ends of the double-edged eyelet together. Turn so the seam is on the inside. Run a gathering thread down the center of the eyelet band. Do not clip the thread. Place the band over the bear's head and slip it down around its neck. Pull the gathering thread, arranging the gathers evenly, until the band fits tightly around the neck. Tie off and clip any excess thread.

15

Tie the ribbon into a bow, trimming off any excess. Stitch the bow to the center of the eyelet. Your bear rag doll is now ready for Baby to play with.

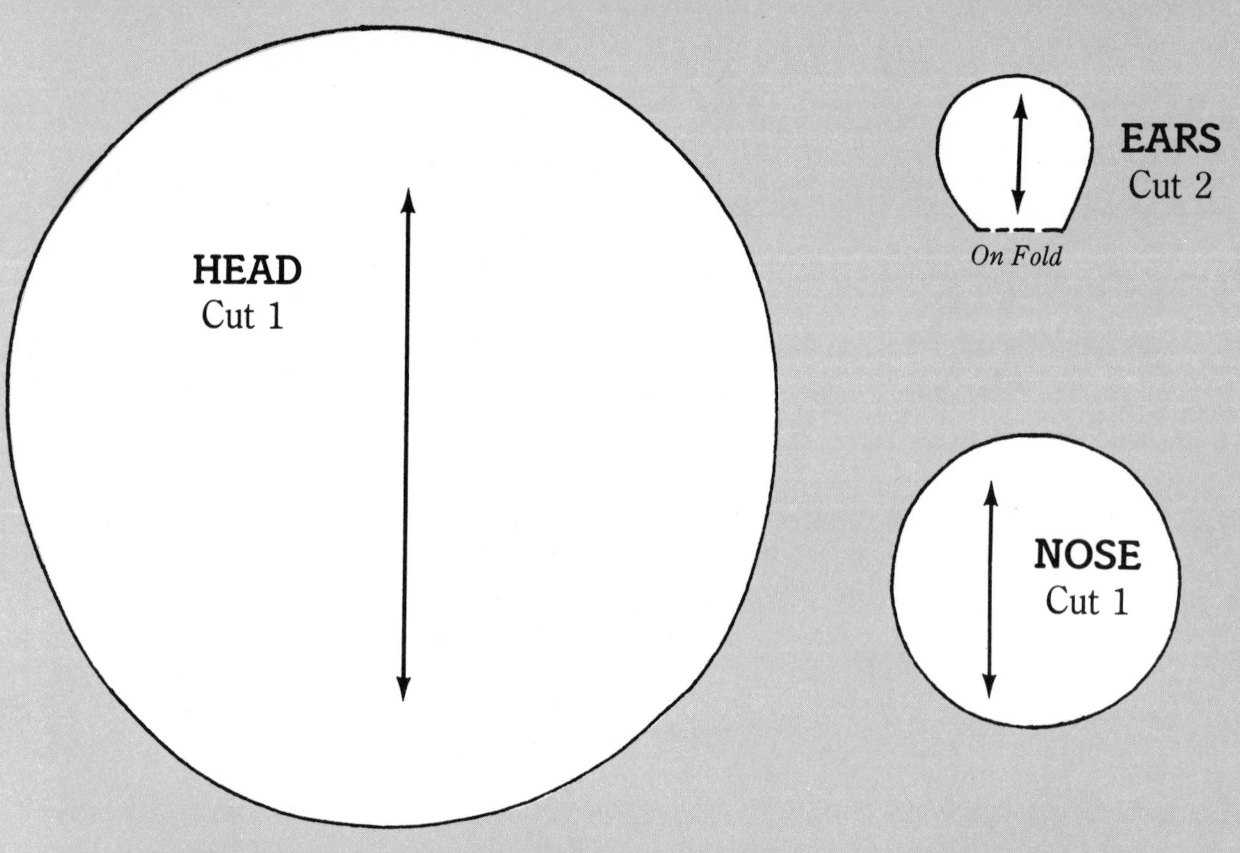

BABY'S RAG DOLL PATTERN

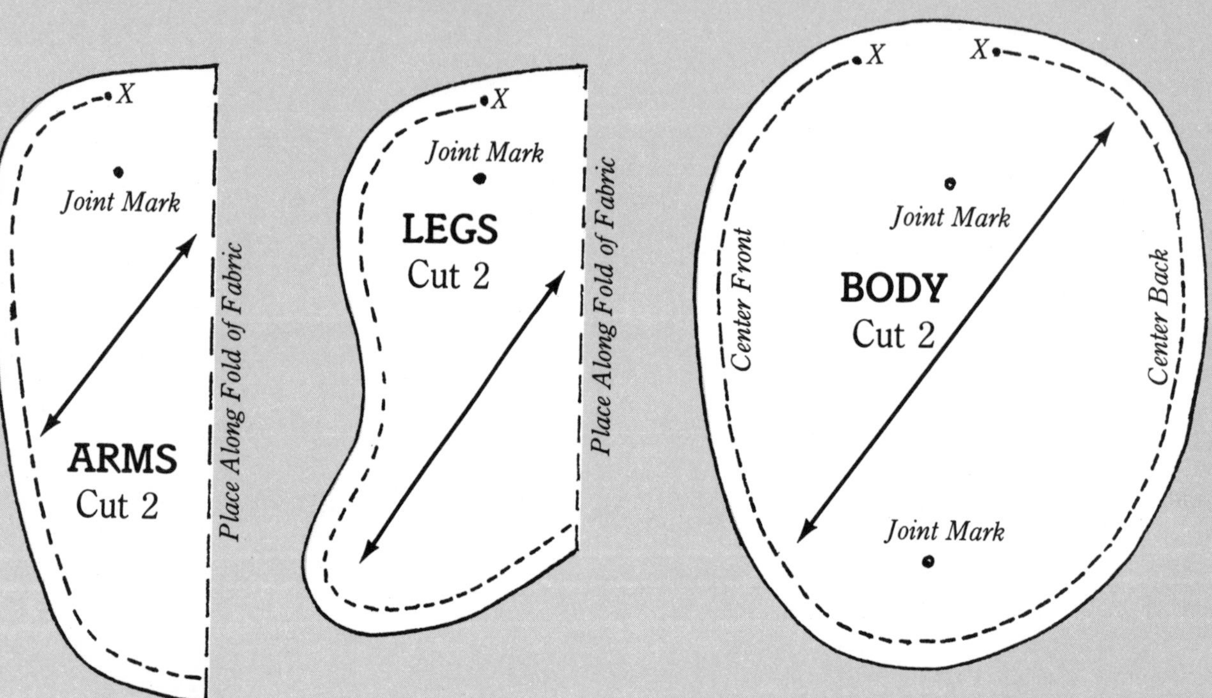

LIVING WITH TEDDY BEARS

BEAR-O-SCOPES

A Teddy Bear is born on the day it is completed, which should be the day its first ribbon is officially tied around its neck.

Because Teddy Bears are uncomplicated creatures with a penchant for simpler things, their astrological charts should all show their signs beginning on the twenty-second day of a month and extending to (not through) the twenty-second day of the following month.

ARIES

BEARTHDAY: March 22 to April 22
INFLUENTIAL PLANET: Mars
FAVORITE COLOR: Red
FAVORITE FLOWER: Honeysuckle
BEARTHSTONE: Aquamarine or diamond

Aries bears are robust. With all their energies, they love living in (or visiting) busy or exciting cities like New York, Philadelphia, Chicago, San Francisco, Los Angeles, and Houston. They thrive on active schedules with multiple activities and enjoy being around people in positions of authority. They do well as companions for business executives.

TAURUS

BEARTHDAY: April 22 to May 22
INFLUENTIAL PLANET: Venus
FAVORITE COLORS: Light pink and light blue
FAVORITE FLOWER: Foxglove
BEARTHSTONE: Diamond or emerald

Taurean bears can be very stubborn, so you must be firm with them from the very beginning. However, they also have unlimited patience and calm, good-natured personalities. They do well when they feel secure, and thrive in rural suburbs, mountain cabins, or rooms with potted plants. If you are a gardener, florist, or farmer a Taurean bear will adapt to your lifestyle.

GEMINI

BEARTHDAY: May 22 to June 22
INFLUENTIAL PLANET: Mercury
FAVORITE COLORS: Yellow and gold
FAVORITE FLOWER: Lily-of-the-valley
BEARTHSTONE: Emerald or pearl

Gemini bears are usually quite trustworthy, intelligent, entertaining and rather flexible. They show no aversion to living amid clutter, disorganization, confusion, and nonroutine lifestyles. They never mind a sudden change in schedule, an impromptu party, a large convention, picnic, vacation or family reunion. Gemini bears bring good luck and companionship to people whose careers are related to writing, radio, television, travel, or politics.

CANCER

BEARTHDAY: June 22 to July 22
INFLUENTIAL PLANET: Moon
FAVORITE COLORS: Grays, silvers and greens
FAVORITE FLOWER: Larkspur
BEARTHSTONE: Pearl or ruby

Cancerian bears are good listeners: sympathetic, compassionate, faithful and loyal. They are generous, devoted to their homes, and their good traits include a strong sense of patriotism. (They love parades.) Cancerian bears have a deep love of the water as well, so they make excellent mascots for boats, swimmers, fishermen, yacht clubs, sailors, and any buildings that house fountains, waterbeds or fish bowls. Cancerian bears do not swim themselves, and are not known for their neatness; if you like everything in order, you will probably have to keep after these bears: they're the type to fall off the shelf or to develop a small hole in a seam and leak stuffing just when you have guests.

LEO

BEARTHDAY: July 22 to August 22
INFLUENTIAL BODY: Sun
FAVORITE COLORS: Sunny yellows and oranges
FAVORITE FLOWER: Sunflower
BEARTHSTONE: Ruby or peridot

Leo bears have a real flair for the dramatic arts; they like to go where the action is, and love any chance to be in the spotlight. Leo bears expect to be revered, are particular about their personal appearance, and enjoy being taken out to dinner or to the theater—or better yet, to both! If people stare because you are walking about with a bear (on the street or at work), remember: It's not *you* they are staring at, but the bear.

VIRGO

BEARTHDAY: August 22 to September 22
INFLUENTIAL PLANET: Mercury
FAVORITE COLORS: Chocolate browns and dark blues
FAVORITE FLOWER: Aster
BEARTHSTONE: Peridot or sapphire

Virgo bears are quite neat and view clutter as distasteful. If you are *not* meticulous, highly organized and orderly, your Virgo bear will always consider you to be hopelessly out of control. When in doubt, bluff it: keep the Virgo bear in the neatest room in the house, and hope it doesn't find out about the rest. On the other hand, Virgo bears are devoted companions.

LIBRA

BEARTHDAY: September 22 to October 22
INFLUENTIAL PLANET: Venus
FAVORITE COLORS: Light shades of pink or blue
FAVORITE FLOWER: Calendula
BEARTHSTONE: Sapphire or opal

Librans are stuffed with charm and have a genuine appreciation for the good life. Libran bears love classical music, soft lights, velvets, silks, lots of ribbons and laces, and an aura of mystery, romance and sophisticated elegance. They have an aversion to arguments, spurn controversy, and prefer a life of peace and quiet, with a little luxury thrown in, of course. Libran bears like to be seen around creative and artistic people (or creative and artistic bears) and may be taken to galleries, ballets, concert halls, museums and the opera.

SCORPIO

BEARTHDAY: October 22 to November 22
INFLUENTIAL PLANET: Pluto
FAVORITE COLOR: Dark red
FAVORITE FLOWER: Chrysanthemum
BEARTHSTONE: Opal or Topaz

Scorpio bears are determined creatures, even to the point of being outrageously stubborn. Scorpios do like to be active and athletic. They are perfectly content to tag along (or observe) when their owners jog, play tennis, climb mountains, ride bicycles, go sailing, go to exercise class, go skating, or take off for a ski weekend. Scorpio bears enjoy attention and wish to be the *only* bear on the bed or shelf. Therefore, if you have many bears, make your Scorpio bear a simple tag that says "They love ME best!," and it will be less apt to sulk.

SAGITTARIUS

BEARTHDAY: November 22 to December 22
INFLUENTIAL PLANET: Jupiter
FAVORITE COLORS: Blues and purples
FAVORITE FLOWER: Narcissus
BEARTHSTONE: Topaz or turquoise

Sagittarian bears are restless and frequently a little careless: they may lose an ear, injure a paw or rip a sweater. They are, however, very adaptable bears and quite willing to exist on a flexible schedule. They are always ready to try exploring or going to a sporting event (a ball game, track meet, skating or swimming competition, tennis or racquetball tournament—or 18 holes of golf).

CAPRICORN

BEARTHDAY: December 22 to January 22
INFLUENTIAL PLANET: Saturn
FAVORITE COLORS: Blacks and grays
FAVORITE FLOWER: Pansy
BEARTHSTONE: Turquoise or garnet

Capricorn bears like to live with the best of everything: they like to wear fine clothes and sit on fine chairs (never shelves). They are determined, motivated, ambitious, and excellent companions for bankers, bookkeepers, school administrators, and retailers of all sorts.

AQUARIUS

BEARTHDAY: January 22 to February 22
INFLUENTIAL PLANET: Uranus
FAVORITE COLOR: Blue
FAVORITE FLOWER: Violet
BEARTHSTONE: Garnet or amethyst

Aquarians are the most faithful, loyal and true of all Teddy Bears. They may see their owners through hospital stays, fires, floods, broken romances, and all sorts of crises. Aquarian bears are very friendly, sincerely compassionate—and good humanitarians.

PISCES

BEARTHDAY: February 22 to March 22
INFLUENTIAL PLANET: Neptune
FAVORITE COLORS: Sea green and lake blue
FAVORITE FLOWER: Water lily
BEARTHSTONE: Amethyst or aquamarine

Piscean bears are simple, kind, gentle, and domestic in nature. They are comfortable in a kitchen, at home in a family room, and are generally content to lead very simple, unassuming lives. They love people, always remain young at heart, and enjoy anything to do with the water. They make fine companions for fishermen, aquarists, swimmers, boaters, and people who enjoy long bubble baths or singing in the shower.

HOW TO NAME YOUR BEARS

How do you name a Teddy Bear? Carefully and with consideration! If everyone just used the first name that came to mind, all the bears in the world would be named "Teddy." That would never do!

A bear should have a special name: one that either suits its face and individual personality, or else enhances its owner's particular tastes, hobbies and personality.

If you choose to name your bear something that suits its looks, try it like this: Sit the bear directly in front of you. Look it straight in the face, nose to nose, and ask (either yourself or the bear), "What is this bear's name?"

It will pop into your mind suddenly that the bear looks just like a Richard, a Robert, a Fluffy—or even an Abercrombie. Some names just fit specific bears; they are appropriate, comfortable to say, and extremely suitable for both owner and bear. On the other hand, there will be times when you should want to be exceptionally clever and creative. When you go to the trouble to make your very own bear, it deserves a special name, perhaps one that fits your special interests, personal qualities or even your career.

FAMILY NAMES

If you have made a complete set of the three bears plus the little rag doll bear toy, you might prefer a quartet of names that are related to each other by subject matter, sound (Percy, Mercy, Hershey and New Jersey) or other means. Naming four-at-a-time like this will also add unity to the bear family itself.

The following names are suggestions that can be used as units of four, or separately for one bear at a time, depending upon your own desires, the number of bears involved and whether or not the bears seem to suggest a single grouping.

For example, do you have a passion for French cooking? How about Bouillabaisse, Vichyssoise, Patisserie and Champignon? Or: Quiche, Crêpe, Croissant and Soufflé? (If you love French, but hate cooking, use François, Pierre, Monique and Jacques.)

Would you prefer something sweeter? Try Chocolate, Marzipan, Peppermint and little Gumdrop. Or, if you're a cheese addict: Brie, Edam, Cheddar, and Gorgonzola. (Their cousins, by the way, might be Cracker, Wafer, Biscuit and Triskit).

Don't forget the berries; they're the best names because they can also be puns if you wish. Berry names make you think of picnics, holidays, country fields and all the wonderful rustic things real bears love.

For berries, pick: Barbeary, Baybeary, Bearbeary, Blackbeary, Bluebeary, Boysenbeary, Candlebeary, Checkerbeary, Cranbeary, Dewbeary (How about Madame Dewbeary?), Elderbeary (for grandbearants, of course), Goosebeary, Hollybeary, Hucklebeary, Juniperbeary, Loganbeary, Mulbeary, Raspbeary, Snowbeary and Strawbeary.

On the other hand, perhaps your bears will be living among automobile enthusiasts. How about Bentley, Mercedes, Porsche and Edsel? Or, for sailing aficionados, there could be Windward, Leeward, Starboard and Port—or the trio Jib, Jenny and Spinnaker. Sportsminded bear owners might like Rugby, Soccer, Lacrosse and Frisbee—or Discus, Shotput, Hurdle and Marathon. (More passive sportspersons might select Checkers, Chess, Cricket and Cribbage—or Backgammon.)

Is someone an art lover? Their bears might be Gainsborough, Matisse, Rembrandt and Renoir. Or a musician? Bearthoven, Bearlioz, Bearahms and Bearnstein.

This could go on indefinitely, but there's still another way to do it. Use the "Appropriate Bear Names" list to create your own combinations. They may also trigger in your mind other names that were on the tip of your tongue but you just couldn't think of till now.

APPROPRIATE BEAR NAMES

Adams	Lancelot
Albert	Larkspur
Amaryllis	Lavender
Arrowroot	Macintosh
Arthur	Madison
Autumn	Merlin
Bard	Minstrel
Barney	Minuet
Beauregard	Mistletoe
Bowler	Molasses
Bumbershoot	Monroe
Buttercup	Napoleon
Calico	Nickelodeon
Calliope	Periwinkle
Candlewick	Petticoat
Candytuft	Pickwick
Carousel	Pomander
Chemise	Porridge
Clover	Potpourri
Coachman	Praline
Crinoline	Ragtime
Edelweiss	Sachet
Footman	Sarsaparilla
Galahad	Sassafras
Gazebo	Spats
Gingham	Steeplechase
Guinevere	Taffeta
Heathcliff	Tapioca
Heather	Tiffany
Honeybunch	Velvet
Ivy	Victoria
Jefferson	Violet
Jester	Wisteria
Josephine	Yak
Kensington	Yarrow
Knickers	Zeke
Lacey	Zinnia

A HOME FOR YOUR BEARS

Where your bears live is a very important matter to consider. First of all, the proper settings enhance bears, make them the focal points of the areas in which they live—and in addition add humor, color, imagination and nostalgia to your own environment.

In choosing a setting, there are many ways to go. You can focus on nostalgia, for instance: Collect antiques or authentic-looking reproductions. A Victorian doll carriage, a wooden cradle, a cutter-type sleigh, doll-size table and chairs, or a basket of any shape or size are among the more desirable objects that convert readily to living quarters for one or more bears.

But antiques of any type can house Teddies comfortably and add an element of surprise that delights both owners and guests, and expresses a personal creativity as well. For instance, a bear peering out from a Victorian umbrella stand or a few of them perched on a melodeon or a hump-backed trunk, are among the arrangements you might try. Vases, coal scuttles and clock cases also make eye-catching living quarters.

A BEAR DEN, OF COURSE

You can also make settings out of almost anything you already own. A wall-mounted knickknack shelf or the bookshelves in a den (pun intended) may be used to display bears either by themselves or with appropriately scaled furniture of your own making or commercially purchased. Large empty wooden thread spools can be painted, stained or "upholstered" to make stools for bears to sit on. Thimbles or bottle caps can be made into drinking mugs, flower vases, dinner plates or candle (birthday cake size) holders. Sponges can be tied or cut into any size or shape and then upholstered with leftover fabric (sometimes even those scraps that match fabrics in the overall room as well) to make lounges, sofas, beds or "sit-upons."

Doll houses, particularly those custom-made to a larger than the common one-inch-to-one-foot scale, also make wonderful settings. (Two-inches-to-one-foot or larger works well if you can construct your setting without crowding yourself out of your own room.)

Bears can also live on a wooden valance over a window. They can add a decorator touch by lounging around on a wicker shelf hanging from a wall in a powder room. An extravagant pedestal soap dish might also be used to display a special bear.

The kitchen is another room where a bear display adds charm. Find one of those multilevel mesh hanging baskets that usually hold fresh fruits and vegetables and substitute a variety of bears—with or without handmade chef's caps or aprons. Very small bears can be shown off in the compartments of a printer's type drawer hung on a kitchen wall, and further filled with miniature pots and pans, artificial foods and any other small items related to bears.

BEARS FOR ANY SEASON

With any setting the accouterments can be changed to fit your mood or the season: orange and black ribbons and small artificial pumpkins for Halloween; red bows, lace and hearts for Valentine's Day; flowers and tiny wooden hand-painted eggs or blown eggshells for Easter; red and green ribbons or Santa hats, bells and pine cones for Christmas; and thin paper streamers and a sprinkling of confetti for New Year's Eve. When you entertain, use bears for a table centerpiece. You might even consider making several of the rag-doll bears on page 101 for place-card holders. What guest wouldn't be delighted with a small personalized bear souvenir to take home after a party?

Small bears also can be used to brighten the trays of children, convalescents, house guests and family members who are being treated to breakfast in bed as a birthday, anniversary or other special surprise. Even a bearthday!

There are no limits to the settings you can improvise for the Teddy Bears you make. The more imagination you use, the better. Through trial and error and occasional searches for new "props" you can create an ever-changing hobby that costs very little.

If you want to go a step further, photograph your various settings and then keep the photographs in a small scrapbook. This will not only give you a record of your artistry, but by reviewing your past work you can create new ideas for other settings.

HOW TO PHOTOGRAPH YOUR BEARS

While Teddy Bears don't close their eyes when the flash goes off, squint in bright sunlight or move after you're all set to snap the picture (well—they do fall over occasionally), they do present special problems when you want to photograph them.

There are a few cardinal rules to follow in order to get the best Teddy Bear photographs, the

most important being to fill up the frame of your picture with the bears or the scene you intend to photograph. (If you have to draw an arrow to point out the bears in your pictures, you didn't get close enough.)

Generally Teddy Bears photograph better indoors than outdoors. Backgrounds are easier to find and conditions are less variable. Lighting is more reliable; shadows can be eliminated more easily or, alternatively, controlled for special effects. Most importantly, your bears won't be overwhelmed by bright sunlight, nor will they get lost in the tall grass.

When working indoors, choose a background which will set off your bear. This may consist of a plain wall or muted background that provides a suitable contrast. Stay away from busy backgrounds with objects, colors or patterns which may distort or detract from the bears.

THE WELL-LIT BEAR

Your next step will be to arrange your lighting. Try to light your bears rather softly to avoid sharp shadows. If you choose to illuminate your bears with a flash, try to bounce the light off the ceiling of the room by pointing your flash upward instead of directly (head on) at the bears. Using the bounce flash technique may require that you open the aperture of your lens more. This can be checked by consulting the flash instructions which come with your camera or flash attachment. Many of the newer electronic flash

attachments, when used with cameras equipped with light metering features, automatically compensate for this bounce technique.

Once you have set your background and lighting, you can set your scene. Keep it simple—bears like it that way.

BRACKET YOUR PHOTOS

Choosing the right camera settings can be a problem. In taking the photos, "bracket" the light settings on your camera if your equipment allows you that flexibility. To do this: Take the first photo with the light setting your light meter (or the film instructions) indicates. Then take a second shot with the lens opened one half-stop more to allow more light in, and a third photo with the lens closed down one half-stop from the original setting. This will allow you a three-way choice in selecting your best shot for later printing, framing or enlarging.

If you are using a camera which allows you no adjustments, you will have to work with as much light as possible and follow the instructions for both camera and film as closely as possible.

While you have your scene still set up, try taking photographs from several different angles. When shooting from directly in front, be careful to avoid giving the bears a distorted look, as the part of the bear nearest the lens may appear larger and out of proportion with the rest of the bear. This same type of distortion can be a problem when you try shooting from above or below the bears. However, if you are careful and take this into consideration, you will be able to minimize the problem.

TAKE CLOSE-UPS OF TEDDY

Now back to that first rule. Fill the frame with your subject matter. At the same time, do not get close enough to inadvertently cut off the paws or the top of the head. The best way to guard against such "photo surgery" is to come in as close as you can, fill the frame of your viewfinder completely with your scene, and then step back about a foot to allow some space around the scene before you finally snap the shutter.

When you are composing a photograph and setting the camera lens, focus on the eyes of your Teddy Bear or some distinct feature other than the fabric in order to make the fine setting of the distance as precise and simple as possible. (Remember: a bear's face is usually the most important feature in a photograph.) Clean the glass or plastic eyes of the bear with a little water, and if you are using floodlights, brighten them with a small dab of petroleum jelly. (Be on your guard against damage which may result to older dried-out or straw-filled bears from the extreme heat of floodlights.)

If all this sounds like hard work, it is. Don't become discouraged. You will have to spend hours crawling around on the floor to take high-quality pictures of Teddy Bears. But the bears won't mind—they seldom get tired of hamming it up and having their pictures taken.

MAIL ORDER SUPPLIERS

Almost everything you need to make your own Teddy Bear is easy to find in a local five-and-ten, craft and notion store. Should you have any trouble locating supplies, the following companies will mail order:

Doll & Craft World, Inc.
125 Eighth Street
Brooklyn, NY 11215
(212) 768-0887
Safety eyes and growler boxes

G. Schoepfer, Inc.
138 West 31 Street
New York, NY 10001
(212) 736-6939 or 736-6934
Complete line of glass eyes

Hersh 6th Avenue Buttons, Inc.
1000 Sixth Avenue
New York, NY 10018
(212) 391-6615
Buttons, seam tape, needles and notions

Janice Naibert
16590 Emory Lane
Rockville, MD 20853
(301) 774-9252
Beautiful silk ribbons, cotton laces and trimmings

Merrily Doll Supply Co.
8542 Ranchito Avenue
Panorama City, CA 91402
(213) 894-0637
Eyes, growlers, fabrics, joint sets, in fact the entire list of materials you will need. Send for their catalog.

Oldebrooke Spinnery
Mountain Road
Lebanon, NJ 08833
(201) 534-2360
Silk twist and natural dyes